Adrian Henri
Selected and Unpubl

Poems 1965–2000

ADRIAN HENRI
SELECTED AND UNPUBLISHED

Poems 1965–2000

edited by
Catherine Marcangeli

with a foreword by
Carol Ann Duffy

LIVERPOOL UNIVERSITY PRESS

First published 2007 by
Liverpool University Press
4 Cambridge Street
Liverpool, L69 7ZU

British Library Cataloguing-in-Publication Data
A British Library CIP Record is available

ISBN 978-1-84631-104-8

Typeset in Dante by Koinonia, Manchester
Printed in Great Britain by Bell & Bain Ltd, Glasgow

Contents

List of Poems

LOVE IS...

HOME AND AWAY

Metropolis

Wish You Were Here

IF YOU WEREN'T YOU...

...Who Would You Like To Be?

TN   'Tonight at Noon and Other Poems', first section of Adrian Henri's *Collected Poems* (Allison and Busby, 1986), comprising works from *The Liverpool Scene* (Rapp and Carroll, 1967), *Penguin Modern Poets No. 10 : The Mersey Sound* (Penguin, 1967 and 1974), *Love Love Love* (Corgi, 1967), *The Best of Henri* (Jonathan Cape, 1975) and *Tonight at Noon* (Rapp and Whiting, 1986), plus two unpublished poems from 1960–1961, 'Death of a Bird in the City' and 'Piccadilly Poems'
CT   *City* (Rapp and Whiting, 1969)
AM   *America* (poems 1969–1970, Turret Books, 1972)
AUT *Autobiography* (Jonathan Cape, 1971)
CH   *City Hedges* (poems 1972–76, Jonathan Cape, 1977)
LM   *From the Loveless Motel* (poems 1976–79, Jonathan Cape, 1980)
PA   *Penny Arcade* (poems 1980–83, Jonathan Cape, 1983)
WY   *Wish You Were Here* (poems 1983–89, Jonathan Cape, 1990)
NFA *Not Fade Away* (poems 1989–1994, Bloodaxe Books, 1994)
LA   *Lowlands Away, an Oratorio for Richard Gordon Smith* (Old School Press, Bath, 2001)
UNP unpublished (translations 1965–2000 and poems 1994–2000)

List of Plates

Foreword

Catherine Marcangeli's magisterial editing of Adrian Henri's *Selected and Unpublished* poems gives back to us a twentieth-century poet whose work touched the lives of ordinary men and women and which was, in its inclusive generosity and engagement, a benign influence on poets, performers, playwrights, artists and musicians over four decades. A 'Liverpool Poet', a wonderful painter, the best of teachers, a natural performer, Henri was born in Birkenhead on 10 April 1932 and died across the Mersey on 20 December 2000. Liverpool was his muse, his source of inspiration, the love of his life, and the city's buildings – from faded Georgian Liverpool 8 to the Pier Head to the two cathedrals at either end of Hope Street – cast their shadows still between the lines of many of his poems.

Adrian Henri was, above all, an enthusiast: for art, landscape, music, travel, football, friendship and romantic love. He was a *bon viveur* whose poems here celebrate, remember and elegise a life bursting at the seams with creative endeavour and passionate participation. Marcangeli's ordering of these poems reveals, like the masterly restoration of an oil painting, the themes and textures of Henri's poetry. The poems glow in their colours afresh. Henri's love poems, even the most well-known, ambush the reader again with their capacity to move. Henri's deep affinity with landscape and nature, with the poems of A. E. Housman, reminds us that he was never a poet who could be pigeon-holed as simply a city poet who knew and loved the works of Apollinaire and Eliot. The deliberately colloquial tone of his work reveals beneath its surface a hugely erudite awareness of the great literary and artistic movements of the nineteenth and twentieth centuries.

On a personal note, I – along with probably hundreds of others – owe a huge debt to Adrian. He selflessly encouraged me, a very young poet, in my writing and made me aware of how important it was to be able to perform one's poetry and to look outwards to the other arts. Perhaps the most remarkable thing about him was his artistic benevolence, his eagerness to absorb, adapt and pass on, and this unique, much-missed sensibility lives and breathes again in this wonderful *Selected and Unpublished*.

Carol Ann Duffy
Manchester, 2007

Introduction

Popular, erudite, lyrical, humorous, sombre at times, Adrian Henri's work presents many facets. I hope this selection does justice to them. It includes works from all periods of Henri's career, from familiar golden oldies such as 'Tonight at Noon', 'Without You' or 'Love Is…', to yet unpublished poems and translations written in the last years of his life.

The poems are divided into three main thematic parts, highlighting Henri's central concerns, and then arranged chronologically within each section, enabling the reader to follow his poetic development.

1. Love Is… Henri is best known as a writer of love poetry. The first section of this volume charts chance encounters, everyday enchantments, false starts, reluctant separations.

2. Home and Away. The second section begins with cityscapes and *flâneurs*, in Liverpool, Manchester or in the heart of some imaginary Metropolis. We then move on to landscapes further afield, with snapshots of Wales, New York or South Africa.Whether he travelled for work, performing his poetry at numerous international festivals, or for pleasure, Henri always brought back 'heaps of broken images', some of which eventually made their way into poems or paintings.

3. If You Weren't You… In Henri's work, homage often takes the form of allusion, parody, variation, direct or buried quotation. The third section opens with poems dedicated to various heroes of his, be they real or imaginary, highbrow or popular. We find Batman cheek by jowl with Liverpool FC legends; Jarry's absurd Ubu Roi with Stéphane Mallarmé and T. S. Eliot; Joseph Cornell and Robert Rauschenberg with James Ensor and Matthias Grünewald; Shostakovich and Debussy with Georges Brassens and Charlie Mingus. This web of references bears witness to Henri's breadth of knowledge and interests, and to his excitement in sharing them. The collection closes on 'straight autobiographical' writing, further emphasizing the fact that Henri was an autobiographical – though not Confessional – poet. He described himself as a 'notebook poet' who constantly jotted down ideas and impressions, exhibitions visited, places discovered. This raw material, once turned into poems, takes on a more universal value, a personal relevance for each and every reader.

Although useful, this division into three parts is of course to a certain extent artificial. The themes overlap and feed off each other. A 'travel' poem can indeed trigger memories of the loved one and musings on the nature of absence, and the landscape suddenly becomes a female body, written in a metre that pays tribute to A. E. Housman's pastoral Shropshire. Henri was well aware of the porosity of such categories when he wrote: 'I'd like to think that if you read through a dozen or so of my poems, which are mostly love poems, you'd be able to say what my views on most political or social or artistic questions were. I'd rather do it this way than write an overtly political poem, or a straight love poem.' These palimpsests create echoes and give texture to his poetry, making our reading experience all the richer, and lasting.

A number of Henri's paintings are reproduced here, and this collection was nearly entitled *I Want to Paint*, after one of his early poems. He trained as a painter, taught at art schools, set up and took part in Happenings in the 1960s and 1970s, while fronting the unlikely poetry-and-rock band Liverpool Scene – prompting John Peel to describe him as 'one of the great non-singers of our time'. He remained a prolific artist, art critic and exhibition curator throughout his writing career. His exploration in both media of the aesthetics of collage is but one of the modes in which the sister arts are interrelated – with the 'New Fast Automatic Daffodils' a canonical example of such playful reactivations of language. *Ut pictura poesis?* Many images indeed crop up in poems and pictures, the different media complementing each other and initiating a thematic and formal dialogue.

The painting of a *Skyline with Swimsuit*, for instance, depicts a simple enough scene, a lover's pink swimsuit left out to dry on a balustrade in a lush California garden. Its poetic companion-piece gives that image a sense of epiphany, turning it into both a love poem and an ironic variation on William Carlos Williams's iconic Modernist 'Red Wheelbarrow'. In *The Entry of Christ into Liverpool in 1964*, the characters face us, static and silent, the frontality of the composition granting the painting a haunting quality equivalent to that of Ensor's original. In the corresponding poem, the description of the scene is anything but static: the familiar linearity of sentences is, on the contrary, disrupted by repetitions and fragmentations, as flashing snippets of a feverish cityscape coalesce to convey a sense of hallucinatory oppression. When performed to music, the poem is more haunting still, its rhythm the stop-and-go heartbeat of a city gasping for breath.

Henri often said how blessed he was that when his poetic muse was feeling lazy, he could go into the studio and find other creative outlets. As Willy Russell puts it in the *Wish You Were Here* section of this volume, Adrian was, in that way as in many, a 'lucky bastard'.

I would like to thank LUP Editorial Director Anthony Cond for giving me the opportunity to put this collection together. My gratitude also goes to Carol Ann Duffy, Roger McGough, Adrian Mitchell, Brian Patten and Willy Russell for their generous contributions, to Frances Pye and Roger Phillips for their precious encouragements, and to all of them for their friendship.

My thanks also, and love, to Adrian Henri, without whom.

Catherine Marcangeli
Liverpool, 2007

LOVE IS ...

24 Collages No. 19, Summer Painting (Père Ubu with Nymphs), 1965

Joyce Collage, 1961

Painting 1, 1972

Skyline with Swimsuit, California, 1992

English Hedge, French Colours, 1998

Love Is …

Whether it is sheep eating yellow roses, ghostly ferries manned by skeleton crews, or prostitutes standing in the snow like erotic snowmen, I've always delighted in Adrian's visual imagination. The poet in him wrote poems containing images that the painter in him wanted to paint, and the painter in him painted images that the poet wanted to write. But really it did not matter which part of his spirit received the images first – Adrian would rush off with them to wherever it is Imagination cooks up its feasts, and, generous as ever, would return to share them with us all.

Brian Patten
Devon, 2007

Love Is …

Love is feeling cold in the back of vans
Love is a fanclub with only two fans
Love is walking holding paintstained hands
Love is

Love is fish and chips on winter nights
Love is blankets full of strange delights
Love is when you don't put out the light
Love is

Love is the presents in Christmas shops
Love is when you're feeling Top of the Pops
Love is what happens when the music stops
Love is

Love is white panties lying all forlorn
Love is a pink nightdress still slightly warm
Love is when you have to leave at dawn
Love is

Love is you and love is me
Love is a prison and love is free
Love's what's there when you're away from me
Love is …

Tonight at Noon[*]

(for Charles Mingus and the Clayton Squares)

Tonight at noon
Supermarkets will advertise 3d EXTRA on everything
Tonight at noon
Children from happy families will be sent to live in a home
Elephants will tell each other human jokes
America will declare peace on Russia
World War I generals will sell poppies in the streets on November 11th
The first daffodils of autumn will appear
When the leaves fall upwards to the trees

Tonight at noon
Pigeons will hunt cats through city backyards
Hitler will tell us to fight on the beaches and on the landing fields
A tunnel full of water will be built under Liverpool
Pigs will be sighted flying in formation over Woolton
and Nelson will not only get his eye back but his arm as well
White Americans will demonstrate for equal rights
in front of the Black House
And the Monster has just created Dr Frankenstein

Girls in bikinis are moonbathing
Folksongs are being sung by real folk
Artgalleries are closed to people over 21
Poets get their poems in the Top 20
Politicians are elected to insane asylums
There's jobs for everyone and nobody wants them
In back alleys everywhere teenage lovers are kissing
in broad daylight

In forgotten graveyards the dead will quietly bury the living
and
You will tell me you love me
Tonight at noon.

*Title taken from an LP by Charlie Mingus, *Tonight at Noon*.

See the Conkering Heroine Comes

Thinking about you
Walking the woods in Autumn
jumping for branches picking glossy horse-chestnuts from the ground
caught purple-handed coming back from blackberrying
Walking handinhand in the summer park
flowers dropping on you as we walk through the palmhouse
magenta to pink to faded rose
pink hearts floating on tiny waterfalls
the woods echoing to the song of the Mersey Bowmen
leaves you said were the colour of the green sweets in Mackintosh's Weekend
cheeks warm and smooth like peaches not apples
hair caught golden in the sunlight
your child's eyes wondering at the colour of rhododendrons
and the whiteness of swans.

Coming back in Autumn
the air loud with the colours of Saturdayafternoon football
the alleyway of trees they planted for us in summer
still there
young appletrees going to sleep in their applepie beds
tropical plants in the palmhouse you said
looked like lions sticking their tongues out
one faded pink flower left
leaves falling very slowly in the tropical afternoon inside
you suddenly seeing a family of mice
living high up in the painted wroughtiron girders.

Walking back
the lakes cold the rhododendrons shivering slightly in the dusk
peacocks closing up their tails till next summer
your hand in mine
the first frost of winter touching your cheeks.

Meat Poem

You skewer through me
bleeding electric
on the brightlylit supermarket counters
of your mind

Car Crash Blues *or* Old Adrian Henri's Interminable
Talking Surrealistic Blues

(for Jim Dine and Ch. Baudelaire)

You make me feel like
someone's driven me into a wall
baby
You make me feel like
Sunday night at the village hall
baby
You make me feel like a Desert Rat
You make me feel like a Postman's hat
You make me feel like I've been swept under the mat
baby

You make me feel like
something from beyond the grave
baby
You make me feel like
Woolworth's After-Shave
baby
You make me feel like a drunken nun
You make me feel like the war's begun
You make me feel like I'm being underdone
baby

You make me feel like
a Wellington filled with blood
baby
You make me feel like
my clothes are made of wood
baby
You make me feel like a Green Shield stamp
You make me feel like an army camp
You make me feel like a bad attack of cramp
baby

You make me feel like
a limestone quarry
baby
You make me feel like
a Corporation lorry
baby
You make me feel like a hideous sore
You make me feel like a hardware store
You make me feel like something spilt on the floor
baby

You make me feel like
a used Elastoplast
baby
You make me feel like
a broken plastercast
baby
You make me feel like an empty lift
You make me feel like a worthless gift
You make me feel like a slagheap shifting
baby

You make me feel like
last week's knickers
baby

You make me feel like
2 consenting vicars
baby
You make me feel like an overgrown garden
You make me feel like a traffic warden
You make me feel like General Gordon
baby
like a hunchback's hump
like a petrol pump
like the girl
    on the ledge
        that's afraid to jump
like a
    garbage truck
        with a heavy load on
           baby

Without You

Without you every morning would be like going back to work after a holiday,
Without you I couldn't stand the smell of the East Lancs Road,
Without you ghost ferries would cross the Mersey manned by skeleton crews,
Without you I'd probably feel happy and have more money and time and
    nothing to do with it,
Without you I'd have to leave my stillborn poems on other people's doorsteps,
    wrapped in brown paper,
Without you there'd never be sauce to put on sausage butties,
Without you plastic flowers in shop windows would just be plastic flowers in
    shop windows,
Without you I'd spend my summers picking morosely over the remains of train
    crashes,
Without you white birds would wrench themselves free from my paintings and
    fly off dripping blood into the night,
Without you green apples wouldn't taste greener,
Without you Mothers wouldn't let their children play out after tea,
Without you every musician in the world would forget how to play the blues,
Without you Public Houses would be public again,
Without you the Sunday Times colour supplement would come out in black-
    and-white,
Without you indifferent colonels would shrug their shoulders and press the
    button,
Without you they'd stop changing the flowers in Piccadilly Gardens,
Without you Clark Kent would forget how to become Superman,
Without you Sunshine Breakfast would only consist of Cornflakes,
Without you there'd be no colour in Magic colouring books,
Without you Mahler's 8th would only be performed by street musicians in
    derelict houses,
Without you they'd forget to put the salt in every packet of crisps,
Without you it would be an offence punishable by a fine of up to £200 or two
    months' imprisonment to be found in possession of curry powder,
Without you riot police are massing in quiet sidestreets,
Without you all streets would be one-way the other way,

Without you there'd be no one not to kiss goodnight when we quarrel,
Without you the first martian to land would turn round and go away again,
Without you they'd forget to change the weather,
Without you blind men would sell unlucky heather,
Without you there would be
no landscapes/no stations/no houses,
no chipshops/no quiet villages/no seagulls
on beaches/no hopscotch on pavements/no night/no morning/there'd be no
        city no country
Without you.

Universes

(for Edward Lucie-Smith)

2 poems for H.P. Lovecraft

1

Miskatonic river
Flowing through a landscape that is always evening
Accusing eyes
in the empty streets of Innsmouth
Strange movements out on the reef
Tumuli on hilltops
Trembling in the thunder
Behind the gambrel roofs of Arkham.

2

'Ph'nglui mgw'nafh Cthulhu R'lyeh wgah'nagl fhtagn'

'In this house at R'lyeh
Great Cthulhu sleeps'

amid
alien geometries
perspectives
walls shifting as you watch them
slumbering
in the Cyclopean dripping gloom
waiting to wake like Leviathan
when his children shall call him.

Four Lovepoems for Ray Bradbury

1

sitting
holding your eight hands
on the bank of the dry red canal

2 *(for Mike Evans)*

you toss your long hair
and look at me with witcheyes

you kiss me
and disappear

my heart bursting
like an April balloon.

3

*'And I'll aways remember
the first time we went out together'*
Your eyes misty behind the glass
Earthlight shining in your hair

4

 the day before the Carnival leaves town.

a shy dwarf
waiting by the boardwalk
for the beautiful dancer
who never comes

Poem for Gully Foyle

'Gully Foyle is my name
Terra is my nation
Deep space is my dwelling place
And Death's my destination'

       Alfred Bester, 'Tiger! Tiger!'

Gouffre Martel. Darkness.
Under the rock and earth a voice
Lying your tigerface blazing in the dark
Listening to her
Your mind still trapped in the broken spaceship

Flaming man appearing like your vengeance
On the beach, in the 3-ring cosmic circus
Your scarred body your tattooed face
Leaping between Aldebaran and Ceres
Eternity at your feet. The stars your destination.

Galactic Lovepoem

(for Susan)

Warm your feet at the sunset
Before we go to bed
Read your book by the light of Orion
With Sirius guarding your head
Then reach out and switch off the planets
We'll watch them go out one by one
You kiss me and tell me you love me
By the light of the last setting sun
We'll both be up early tomorrow
A new universe has begun.

Adrian Henri's Talking After Christmas Blues

Well I woke up this mornin' it was Christmas Day
And the birds were singing the night away
I saw my stocking lying on the chair
Looked right to the bottom but you weren't there
there was
      apples
        oranges
          chocolate
            … aftershave
– but no you.

So I went downstairs and the dinner was fine
There was pudding and turkey and lots of wine
And I pulled those crackers with a laughing face
Till I saw there was no one in your place
there was
      mincepies
        brandy
          nuts and raisins
            … mashed potato
– but no you.

Now it's New Year and it's Auld Lang Syne
And it's 12 o'clock and I'm feeling fine
Should Auld Acquaintance be Forgot ?
I don't know girl, but it hurts a lot
there was
      whisky
        vodka
          dry Martini (stirred
            but not shaken)
              … and 12 New Year resolutions
- all of them about you.

So it's all the best for the year ahead
As I stagger upstairs and into bed
Then I looked at the pillow by my side
 … I tell you baby I almost cried
there'll be
            Autumn
                Summer
                    Spring
                        … and Winter
– all of them without you.

Nightsong

So we'll go no more a-raving
So late into the night
Though the heart be still as loving
And the neonsigns so bright

Ate my breakfast egg this morning
playing records from last night
woke to hear the front door closing
as the sky was getting light

No more fish-and-chips on corners
Watching traffic going by
No more branches under streetlamps
No more leaves against the sky

No more blues by Otis Redding
No more coffee no more bread
No more dufflecoats for bedding
No more cushions for your head

Though the night is daylight-saving
And the day returns too soon
Still we'll go no more a-raving
By the light of the moon

Who?

Who can I
spend my life
with
Who can I
listen to Georges Brassens
singing
'Les amoureux des bancs publics'
with
Who can I
go to Paris with
getting drunk at night with
tall welldressed spades
Who can I
quarrel with
outside chipshops
in sidestreets
on landings
Who else
can sing along with Shostakovitch
Who else
would sign a Christmas card
'Cannonball'
Who else
can work the bathroom geyser
Who else
drinks as much bitter
Who else
makes all my favourite meals
except the ones I make
myself
Who else
would bark back at dogs
in the moonlit lamplight streets

Who else
would I find
waiting dark bigeyed
in a corner of a provincial jazzclub
You say
we don't get on
anymore
but
who can I
laugh on beaches with
wondering at the noise
the limpets make
still sucking in the tide
Who
can I
buy
my next Miles Davis record
to share with
who
makes coffee the way I like it
and
love the way I used to like it
who
came in from the sun
the day
the world went spinning away
from me
who doesn't wash the clothes I always want
who
spends my money
who
wears my dressing gown
and always leaves the sleeves turned up
who
makes me feel
as empty as the house does

when she's not there
who
else
but
you

For Joyce

Love from Arthur Rainbow

In a villa called 'Much Bickering'
In a street called Pleasant Street
Living with her wicked parents
Was a princess, small and neat

She wanted to be an artist
So off to college she went
And as long as she got a Diploma
They considered it money well spent

One day she met a poet
Who taught her all about life
He walked her down to the station
Then went back home to his wife

He came from the end of the rainbow
At least that's what she thought
The kind of love she wanted
The kind that can't be bought

But time and the last train to the suburbs
Killed the love that would never die
And he'll find another love
And she'll sit at home and cry

Now she's reading through his letters
In her small schoolteacher flat
Dusty paint-tubes in the corner
Worn-out 'Welcome' on the mat

O the day she met Arthur Rainbow
There were roses all over town
There were angels in all the shopwindows
And kisses not rain coming down

Now it's off to work every morning
And back home for dinner at eight
For the gold at the end of the rainbow
Lies buried beneath her front gate.

In the Midnight Hour

When we meet
in the midnight hour
country girl
I will bring you nightflowers
coloured like your eyes
in the moonlight
in the midnight
hour

I remember

Your cold hand
held for a moment among strangers
held for a moment among dripping trees
in the midnight hour

I remember

Your eyes coloured like the autumn landscape
walking down muddy lanes
watching sheep eating yellow roses
walking in city squares in winter rain
kissing in darkened hallways
walking in empty suburban streets
saying goodnight in deserted alleyways

in the midnight hour

Andy Williams singing 'We'll keep a Welcome in the Hillsides' for us
When I meet you at the station
The Beatles singing 'We can Work it Out' with James Ensor at the harmonium
Rita Hayworth in a nightclub singing 'Amade Mia'
I will send you armadas

of love vast argosies of flowers
in the midnight hour
country girl

when we meet

in the
moonlight
midnight
hour
country girl

I will bring you

yellow
white
eyes
bright
moon
light
mid
night
flowers
in the midnight hour.

Song for a Beautiful Girl Petrol-Pump Attendant on the Motorway

I wanted your soft verges
But you gave me the hard shoulder.

Permissive Poem

'Oh mummy dear' the daughter said
Dropping her silver spoon
'*Please* don't say dirty weekend
We call it our mini-moon.'

Love Poem

(*for Sidney Hoddes*)

'I love you' he said
With his tongue in her cheek.

Cat Poem

You're black and sleek and beautiful
What a pity your best friend won't tell you
Your breath smells of Kit-E-Kat.

I Suppose You Think It's Funny

I suppose you think it's funny
when your smile opens me like a tin of Kit-E-Kat
I suppose you think it's funny
when perfumed dancers with sequinned tights
fill my Arabian Nights with Turkish Delights
I suppose you think it's funny

when your nightdress falls open revealing last year's election posters
I suppose you think it's funny
to post the cat and put out my poems instead
I suppose you think it's funny
to hang a photograph of Eichmann over your bed
signed *'Affectionately yours, Adolf'*
I suppose you think it's funny
when the bath breaks out in limegreen spots before my astonished gaze
I suppose you think it's funny
to give away the time we've spent to a door-to-door Ancient of days
I suppose you think it's funny
to publish my secret identity in the *Liverpool Echo*
I suppose you think it's funny
to fill my Y-fronts with Red Kryptonite
I suppose you think it's funny
to comb your hair like a lion
and push my breakfast through the bars
I suppose you think it's funny
to fill the next door garden with schoolgirls playing guitars
I suppose you think it's funny
when I cover you with flowers
I suppose you think it's funny
when you take an April shower
I suppose you think it's funny
when you've taken all my money
and the bailiff's in the parlour
eating bread and honey
and you meet me in a thunderstorm
and tell me that it's sunny
I suppose *you* think it's funny.

Poems for Wales

1   icegreen
      mountain streams
        fresher
          than toothpaste
           cleaner tasting
             than menthol cigarettes.

2   Gelert's grave
   used to make me cry like a baby
   now
   they're killing Vietnamese
   instead

3   standing
   looking at the landscape
   then
   signing it at the bottom
   in the snow on a petrol-station wall

4   thinking about you
   here
   in the country
   trying to spray the moon silver
   and
   only hitting the clouds

5   two lots of footprints
   through the snow
   to my room
   both of them
   mine

Country Song

'Lily of the Valley (Convalaria Majalis, fam. Liliaceae). Grows wild in N. England. Commonly cultivated. Flowers in May. Berries red when ripe. Leaves particularly poisonous because three constituents depress the heart, like Foxglove.'

What are the constituents that depress the heart?
the scent of lilies in darkgreen silences under trees
milkweed and ragwort and sunshine in hedges
small flowers picked amongst trees when it's raining

A year ago
You planted lilies in the valley of my mind
There were lilies at the bottom of my garden
And ferries at the bottom of my street

Now
I sit here in sunlight with the smell of wild garlic
Trying to taperecord the sound of windflowers and celandines

Wondering
What are the three constituents that depress the heart
Without you here in the country?

Song of Affluence *or*
I Wouldn't Leave My 8-Roomed House for You

I wouldn't leave my little 8-roomed house for you
I've got one missus and I don't want two

I love you baby but you must understand
That feeling you's fine and kissing you's grand
But I wouldn't leave my little wooden wife for you

Water tastes fine but money tastes sweeter
I'd rather have a fire than a paraffin heater
And
I wouldn't change my little 8-roomed life for you.

Where'er You Walk

'Where'er you walk
Cool gales shall fan that glade'

The Pierhead where you walked will be made a park
restricted to lovers under 21
Peasants will be found merrymaking after the storm in Canning St
where you walked
The station where we first arrived at night
Will be preserved for the nation
With the echo of your footsteps still sounding in the empty roof

'Where'er you tread
The Blushing flower shall rise'

The alleyway where we read poems to dustbins
after closing time
The kitchens where we quarrelled at parties
The kitchen where two strangers first kissed at a party
full of strangers
The ticketbarrier where we said goodnight so many times
The cobblestones in front of the station
The pub where the kindly old waiter
Always knows what we want to drink –
ALL SHALL BURST INTO BLOOM
SPROUTING FLOWERS BRIGHTER THAN PLASTIC ONES IN
      WOOLWORTH'S
Daffodils and chrysanthemums, rhododendrons and snowdrops, tulips and roses
– cobblestones bursting with lilies-of-the-valley

'And all things flourish'

Whole streets where you walk are paved with soft grass
so the rain will never go through your shoes again
Zebracrossings made of lilies
Belishabeacons made of orangeblossom
Busstops huge irises
Trafficlights made of snapdragons

'Trees where you sit
Shall crowd into a shade'

even in Piccadilly
stations covered in flowers yellow like the paint you once got in your hair
Oaktrees growing everywhere we've kissed
Will still be there when I've forgotten what you look like
And you don't remember me at all
Copies of your letters to me on blue paper
Written on the sky by an aeroplane over all the cities of england
Copies of your poems stamped on eggs instead of lions
We will walk forever in the darkness of fernleaves

'Trees where you sit
shall crowd into a shade'

from City, Part One

Got up went to the telephone bought some pies and rolls for
    lunch thinking of you tried to phone you they said you
    weren't there came home made some coffee had my lunch
    thinking of you.

Got washed put stuff under my arms to make me smell nice
    thinking of you got shaved put on aftershave to make me
    smell nice thinking of you listened to a record of Pannalal
    Ghosh playing the flute went out into the dry city afternoon
    thinking of you thinking of you.

Waking up with a headache from the night before thinking of
    you feeling suddenly sick not knowing where you are no
    way of talking to you no way of hearing from you Andy
    thinking I'd written a Haiku without knowing it and then
    discovering I hadn't.

Listening to Nadia sing 'All My Trials, Lord' in the spotlit
    church darkness thinking about the fresh downycheeked
    slightly blushing still schoolgirl girl who used to sing it four
    years ago still thinking of you.

Looking from the train window going small green fields
    glimmering like a pond with lapwings golden down on the
    mountainsides against a pale blue sky thinking of you
    coming back orderly rows of firtrees small rows of round
    trees fading into the horizon toy cars running up an
    inclined slope into the mist seeing wet platforms in Carlisle
    thinking of you sky and embankment covered with ferns
    and brambles grey seen through a green filter writing this
    poem thinking of you thinking of you.

Waking and reaching out in the early morning for the warm
    bigeyed girl who called everyone a machine and whose full
    breasts were a sleeping machine and whose big warm
    mouth was a kissing machine and whose hot suddenly

wanting morning body a love machine I couldn't control
still thinking of you.

Drinking whisky with Hamish after a quarrel in the illicit
sundaymondaymorning hours listening to song after Celtic
song thinking of you eating a farewell meal with John and
Lucy in the latenight café we go to every night thinking of
you.

Listening to Adrian telling me about the lies they tell me about
Vietnam thinking of you thinking about the napalmed
children not flower children but innocent flowers of flame
listening to a piper playing 'Lament for the Children'
listening to Simpson playing pibroch 'Dargai' wondering
why I can't write a lament for the firechildren of Vietnam as
beautiful as the haunted landscape music echoing from
peak to peak and range to range of sound across glens of
silence ageless lament of the mothers for the children of the
first 'pacification'.

Listening to Mike read listening to Alan and Pete Morgan
listening to my friends tell me the truth thinking of you
listening to Ted Joans laughing spade hero hipster black
flower from Africa feeding the audience poems songs
chocolate and astonishment thinking of you thinking of
you.

Thinking of you in the 2 a.m. slightly drunk darkness at the
top of the hill with Jim and Andy seeing old and new town
spread out in points of light beneath us under the towering
stonehenge Doric columns the sound of a flute breaking
into the still air Bartok and Debussy moving out over the
lamplit streets all night railwaystation and sleeping town.

Thinking of you drinking in the latenight empty hotel lounge
with Patrick newlymet friend but familiar face from the
telly making takeover bids for the songs of Catullus and
power struggles for control of Virgil's 'Georgics'.

Thinking of you trying to finish this poem back in Liverpool
where everyone's my friend except some of my friends
taking the flower painting I did for you to be framed in gold
like our love should be thinking of you trying to finish this
poem at the seaside walking with the dog along the early
September already winter promenade where we walked a
year ago thinking of you trying to finish this poem walking
in the country a few late flowers and blackberries in the
hedges the hills ahead 'the spectre of repopulation'
waiting huge hawkheaded just behind the skyline.

Thinking of you then one day an unexpected phone call in the
afternoonlunchtimedrinking helping another girl to buy flowers
afternoon hearing your familiar halfforgotten voice sad but
still warm faraway saying you can't see me walking home
with no mac and my shoes are sneakers and let the rain in
everyone over 30 has shoes and an overcoat except me
feeling the still warm September rain soaking through my
clothes thinking of you thinking of you.

Thinking of you watching Magic Roundabout me here and
you miles away hoping Florence and the boys will look after
you Dougal will trip over himself trying to help Mr
McHenry will bring you flowers but Zebedee doesn't tell us
'time for bed' anymore.

Walking through dead leaves in Falkner Square going to the
Pakistani shop with Tony in the October afternoon
sunlight thinking of you being woken up in the two a.m.
Blue Angel rockn'roll darkness by Carl who I hadn't heard
singing thinking of you thinking of you drinking in the
Saturday night everyone waiting no party pub walking
with another girl holding cold hands in the autumn park
thinking of you walking home everynight in Blackburne
Place twilight thinking of you thinking of you.

Morning Song

Of meat and flowers I sing
Butchers and gardeners:

When aware of the body's process
The long journey into red night
The unfamiliar pounding that may cease at any moment
Drift off into the night full of sounds
Ticklings and murmurs, whispers and gurglings

When my mouth
Open against the open world of you
Into the darkness of rosepetals
Continents against white continents
Shudder in perspective

When the curtains are drawn
And you blossom into morning
Eyes unveiled from sleep flower-beds thrown back
White lilies against your hair's vine-leaves
I will rise and moisten the warm wet soil
to perfection

Of meat and flowers I sing
Butchers and gardeners:
Songs thrown bleeding onto counters
Reaching up to the sun through city backyards.

Wartime

1   Hostage
(in memoriam Ulrike Meinhof)

Urban Guerrilla
you burst into me
machinegunned
the old poems
stationed at the door
for just such a contingency
made off
with my heart
in the getaway car
despite
a desperate chase
by police in armoured cars
held it to ransom
demanding
nothing less than total involvement.

That night
a bloodless revolution
statues of the old regime
toppled in the streets
victory-fires
lit on every hillside.

Now,
in the final shootout
you fight on alone
at the window of the blazing house
I a voluntary hostage
bewildered
listen to the howl
of approaching squad-cars

taste
the stench of gas-grenades
as the masked militiamen
burst
into the room
wonder
if I'll miss you.

2   Regime

Torn posters flap
wind howls through
rusting hustings
no fate is known
for those deposed
brave new politicians
govern the bedroom
undisturbed by the sound
of distant firing-squads.

3   Truce

After the bitter end of war
and tired troops return
wounded sunbathe
hospital-blue on balconies
retreat
my undefeated lover

starshells will wake us
mysterious armies
regroup by night
between our separate bodies
tomorrow
the dawn attack
the blood-filled trenches
worlds locked again
in loving combat.

Scenes from the Permissive Society

1   There were no survivors from the dawn raid …
(for Richard Hill)

Soldiers of love:
returning at dawn
shock-troops
in the sex-war
dropped
2 doors away
no prisoners taken
cyanide button sewn onto lapel
excuses timed
with a self-destruct mechanism
activated
at the first sign of tears.

2   Poem to be printed on a pair of paper panties

Throw these away in the morning
Like the things we said last night
Words that go bump in the darkness
Crumpled and stained in the light

Promises made with our bodies
Dropped in the bin by the day
Look for the signs of our loving
Carefully hide them away

Straighten the folds in the bedclothes
Smooth out the pillow we shared
Tidied away in the corner
Along with our last lying words.

3

I want a love
as intimate as feminine deodorant
As easily disposed of
as paper underwear
As fresh as
the last slice of sliced bread
As instant as
flavour-rich coffee granules
As necessary as
money
Available
on demand
A love
as glossy
double-spread
full-colour
full-frontal
as a Bunny-girl
(and the only key
belongs to me)

I want a
Number One
Smooth creamy
Hi-speed
Cross-your-Heart
Getaway
Cool as a
Cosy-Glo
Fingertip control
Throwaway
Here today
Never pay
Any way
love.

Evening Song

'I will come to you when the light has gone …'

I will come to you when the light has gone
When the sea has wandered far from its shores
And the hedges are drenched in evening
I will come to you when the light is gone

I will come to you when the day has gone
When butterflies disappear in the dark
And the night is alive with tiny wings
I will come to you when the day is gone

I will come to you when the night has come
And morning-glories swell in the darkness
Birds lie wrapped in nests of silence
I will come to you when the night is come

I will love you till the day has come
Trees and fields revealed in morning
Birds awake and sing the sunrise
I will love you till the day is come.

Lullaby

Here is a poem written on the clouds for you
When white bodies dance in suburban gardens
Accompanied only by the sound of lawnmowers
Champagne pouring into empty swimming-pools
Here is a poem written on the clouds for you

Here is a poem written on the sky for you
On the very last day
When skulls and hummingbirds crowd the beaches like deckchairs
Seagulls singing their final requiem
Here is a poem written on the sky for you

Here is a poem written in the air for you
When the flood is over
And pigs are left dangling in the treetops
Valleys overturned and rivers upended
Here is a poem written in the air for you

Here is a poem written on the clouds for you
When the poets are gone and the poems forgotten
When a new earth blooms
And the dying heart pumps a song of welcome
Here is a poem written on the clouds for you.

Three Landscapes

1

pledged
by the wild plum-tree
kisses
only a bite away
childhood
silence
alive with gossamers.

2

red earth
stillness
lane shuttered
high
above
the sound of ash trees.

3

Dalmatian dog
spotted
against painted glass
your hair
harvested with sunlight.

A Song for A. E. Housman

I walk the lanes of Wenlock
And dream about the night
Where every leaf is shrivelled
And every berry bright

In Wenlock Town the drink goes down
The laughter flows like wine
In Wenlock Town the leaves are brown
And you're no longer mine

Day turns to night in Wenlock
Laughter to early tears
Down by the hill I follow still
The path we walked this year

Come let it snow on Wenlock
Fall down and cover me
Happy I was in Wenlock
Happy no more I'll be.

Butterfly

(for Carol Ann Duffy)

cry
for the butterfly
in your warm hand
hard light
on the threadbare tapestry of my wings
rainbow dust
left on the loved lines
of your palm

cry
with me
helpless
pinned against
stark white
black writing

sing
of your gift
for your lover
as I fall
flicker against your feet

sing
as I die
caught between intricate syllables
your song
pierce my body
butterfly
flutters
at the foot of the page
tiny rainbow
dies for your song
in the evening sunlight.

Don't Look

Don't look in my eyes, then
look at the dragonflies
glittering   look at the river

Don't listen to my words
listen to the crickets
loud in the hayfield   listen to the water

Don't touch me
don't feel my lips   my body
feel the earth alive with sedges
trefoil valerian   feel the sunlight

My lady,
these things I bring you
don't see   only know
a landscape in your body
a river in my eyes

Autumn Leaving

1
dead leaves
drift through your words
cold winds
blow between sentences
eddy between paragraphs
wet leaves flat
in the backyard of our love.

I am fed up with you hanging out your words
on the washing-line of my life
my dirty linen for your public

between
between your
wet alleyways your dead
wasteland trees
not growing in the lamplight
dark spaces between the lines
and your words don't tell
how our city is empty and
how for seven years
bound to you syllable by syllable
street by street paragraph by paragraph.

I shall no longer wait for the telephone
to tell me the poems you write for others
nor wash your lies from the kitchen floor

our love
as silent as words
as noisy as backyards
as desolate as sentences.

I shall no longer clean this bedroom
other women's words snug beneath your pillow
the bedclothes stiff with adjectives

away from you
here
in this abandoned valley
drifts of dead nouns
drowned verbs
hills spread apart
rich orange-red slopes
brazen to the sky
to the sound of you still
on the tip of my tongue.

I will no longer
Hoover the corners of our life
nor
lie back and let you
bury your words in me

words apart
and only the streetlights between us
waiting these years
between lamplight and morning.

2
Onion in December

an onion in December
layers of words
plump with unshed tears
and stored sunlight
waiting on the shelf
for your winter knife.

3
Spring Ending

and
tomorrow
students
will lay gentle flowers
on the bloodstained pavement
where our relationship died
last night.

4
Full and Frank

At summit conferences
we argue
about custody of the deodorant
and visiting hours for the cat
at weekends. Fair shares
of the wallpaper
and last year's European Cup programme.

A pillowcase
a dusty sugar pig
and two dog-eared cookery books
lurk
on the agenda.
Our tears
wait
under Any Other Business.

5
Morning Two

waking
and reaching out for you
in the curtained light
the empty space beside me
throbs the stump of our love
a phantom limb
beneath the bedclothes.

6
Robins

Christmas cards come
addressed to the two of us
I wonder
shall I tear them in half?
send you the robins?
keep the holly?

7
Cenotaph

In this corner
of a foreign girl
I suddenly remember how
the smell of TCP
used to excite me
nightly,
how
we came close and then slept.

Now
at dawn
a bugle sounds
I whisper excuses
and, leaving,
lay a wreath upon the pillow.

'At the going down of the drawers,
And in the morning,
We will remember them.'

8
Pressing the wings of butterflies for paper
I write you poems at midnight.
Their small, still, silent voices
Echo my words.

Red Card

Right from the off,
straight into your penalty area
a quick one-two and it was all over
bar the shouting. Easy
Easy sang the terraces.

Half-time: I've given you a hundred per cent
and more. Two down, and I've got it all
to do again.

At the end of the day
the lap of honour. Your ribbons
round the Cup. I am
sick as a parrot. I am
over the moon you tell the cameras,
the waiting millions.
Back home I walk
alone.

What Shall We Do with the Drunken Poet?

Thinking of you
On a waterbed
Feeling
Seasick with jealousy.

Moon-Clover

Black-hearted clover
away from our sight
Why do you blossom
only at night?

Why do you bloom
as the moon fills the sky?
Why do you flourish
away from our eye?

Black-hearted moon-clover
shunning the day
Remember the field
where my love and I lay.

Train Windows

1
I think of you
in a blue dawn
tractor against the horizon
garlanded with seagulls
orange sun
across frosted fields.

2
thin snow on the mountains
guillemots on empty beaches
the sea lying placid
white as milk in a blue saucer.

3
woods
dark as your eyes
white birds against flooded fields
red-brown water
lapping round railway lines.

4
dusk streams
and the late cries of sea-birds
last light through trees
blue tents of camps where bugles fall
before the busy dark.

Any Prince to Any Princess

August is coming
and the goose, I'm afraid,
is getting fat.
There have been
no golden eggs for some months now.
Straw has fallen well below market price
despite my frantic spinning
and the sedge is,
as you rightly point out,
withered.

I can't imagine how the pea
got under your mattress. I apologize
humbly. The chambermaid has, of course,
been sacked. As has the frog footman.
I understand that, during my recent fact-finding tour of the Golden River,
despite your nightly unavailing efforts,
he remained obstinately
froggish.

I hope that the Three Wishes granted by the General Assembly
will go some way towards redressing
this unfortunate recent sequence of events.
The fall in output from the shoe-factory, for example:
no one could have foreseen the work-to-rule
by the National Union of Elves. Not to mention the fact
that the court has been fast asleep
for the last six and a half years.
The matter of the poisoned apple has been taken up
by the Board of Trade: I think I can assure you
the incident will not be
repeated.

I can quite understand, in the circumstances,
your reluctance to let down
your golden tresses. However
I feel I must point out
that the weather isn't getting any better
and I already have a nasty chill
from waiting at the base
of the White Tower. You must see
the absurdity of the situation.
Some of the courtiers are beginning to talk,
not to mention the humble villagers.
It's been three weeks now, and not even
a word.

Princess,
a cold, black wind
howls through our empty palace.
Dead leaves litter the bedchamber;
the mirror on the wall hasn't said a thing
since you left. I can only ask,
bearing all this in mind,
that you think again,

let down your hair,

reconsider.

The Business

It's always men who do you wrong
So why not make them pay?
You'll find a friend who'll put you wise
Why give it all away?

The ship girl

The last one was a Dutchman, the one tonight's a Greek
It's just like being married but it only lasts a week
And then it's down the House of Sin to find another one
I wish I could just sail away and no one know I've gone.

O Brothers, tell your sisters
Not to go where I have been
Spending my life with sailormen
Down in the House of Sin.

The massage girl

You'd like to do so many things
Your wife won't understand
Lie down, we'll soothe your cares away
Just leave it in our hands.

The call girl

My grandma walked down Lime Street
And they called her Maggie May
But my name is Michelle
And things are different today.
A contact girl, a contract girl,

With candlelight and wine,
Just dial my number any time
The pleasure will be mine.

The street girl

Upper Parly's cold and wet
It's colder in the Square
I'm here beneath the lamplight
You can always find me there.

When he left me I was six months gone
So what's a girl to do?
I never got my CSEs
All I can do is screw.

It's the oldest game a girl can play
This every woman knows
By day and night, in rain or snow,
The business doesn't close.

In hotel lounge or on the street,
A cabin or a car,
A photo on a glossy page,
You need us: here we are.

Seaside

dawn chorus:

Like angels awaiting some fishy nativity
in the lace-curtain light
hosts, perspectives of seagulls fill the sky
shriek and gibber
I lie like leather in whatever stone you choose to set
their raucous cries fill my head
like the sheeted dead
you stir in your sleep
away from me.

2

Gaily painted pleasure-streamers
ply their trade between us
from my headland I scan, anxiously,
the expected messenger is not
in any of their argosies.

3

The sea has carefully mislaid the beach
beyond our reach. It looks like rain.
Over the boardwalk bridge we trace in vain
your lost shell earring – remembered image
of harbour, swans, and rainbow – gone, perhaps
back to its watery element.

We examine its green brothers in the Shell Shop
and do not find its like. Its lack
as tangible as absent-minded station kisses.
Your eyes as distant, clouded
as the sea in its remote horizon.

4

We sit on the pier and talk of growing old.
A seagull wheels, agelessly. The sea
moves restlessly from right to left. Before
the fishermen cast their lines. Behind, the dodgem-cars
are tuning up. BINGO. SOUVENIRS. The painted shapes
of clouds unreal as candy floss. The distance gapes
wide as the emerald gap beneath the planks,
between our feet.

5

There was, I remember, something about a harbour.
And, yes, a rainbow and – what was it?
Swans, yes, that was it, swans – laughing
we pass unnoticing the window. Our sepia faces
frozen, helpless.

Aubade

I mourn for something that was never there
Remind myself of times a year ago:
The scent of roses in the morning air.

In this small room the senses all declare
You were with me, my love, and yet I know
I mourn for something that was never there.

Mist hides the hills, the season is so unfair,
Left here I sit and watch the summer go,
The scent of roses in the morning air.

Bees can't resist the honeysuckle's snare.
Frantic as they are, clumsy and far too slow
I mourn for something that was never there.

Thoughts of your eyes, the morning in your hair,
Lost like a leaf against the river's flow,
The scent of roses in the morning air.

Time will not stop: your careless hand will tear
The faded snapshot, all that was left to show.
I mourn for something that was never there,
The scent of roses in the morning air.

Dial-a-Poem

a poem
instead of a phone call
a jewel
exchanged
for a green apple
or an empty station
two minutes
of silence
away from the red-framed world
outside

a song
for a kiss
a kiss
for an apple
an apple
for a jewel
a jewel
for a poem
a poem
instead of a phone call
I didn't make
last night.

At Your Window

proudly I present
a dead mouse
at your window
dismembered birds
at the kitchen door
cannot believe
do not conceive
your horror
at the gifts I bring you.

Evensong

I write you poems in dayglo colours.
You hold them against the sunset
and tell me you cannot read them.

Caller

In the time between
they pick it up
and put it down
I do it.
Quick syllables
slither down the line
like a hand up a skirt
on an escalator.
Sometimes I can hear
a little gasp of puzzlement
or fear. That's the best time.
Easy to please, that's me.
All it takes to satisfy
is 10p.

Hotel

Amid tropical decor
they laugh in evening dress
and speak of markets, of orders lost
and gained. I sit
in my fluorescent scarf and socks
as fans revolve overhead
and try to graph the ebb and flow
of your feelings, anticipate
the profit and loss of our loving.

Friday Morning, Early October

'One thing might lead
to another'
you say. 'Better not meet
another day'. On the morning
telephone. Alone,
and wondering,
what thing led us
to one another. What thing
will lead you to another.

Ophelia

'There's rosemary, that's for remembrance:
pray you, love, remember …'

It is the painting I will not now paint for you.
Lying back in the upstairs bathroom
warm pink in a haze of warm water,
green with the essence of horse-chestnuts,
like the leaves hanging over her river.
1851, and in a golden summer
a man paints blue-flags, dog-roses, a robin
perched on a twig. Nearby, his friend paints a cornfield
not yet occupied by lovers. A willow dreams
aslant a brook. Look deep into the green world
of pondweed. In winter he will paint her
dress enchanted with tiny ornaments in a bathtub
in London. In Liverpool you would have floated
breasts above the water, pubic hair tangled
like water-crowfoot. Later I would have painted you
a Devon riverbank alive with dragonflies, valerian.
Viridian depths. This is the painting I would have made for you

my dark-haired, full-bodied Ophelia. But you are gone
and the image floats away downstream as shadows gather
in the green-carpeted bathroom. The lily-pads
of the bathmat you gave me remember.

For Joyce

'I don't want
to be any trouble' you'd say,
every day. 'Don't want
to be any trouble'. If you don't want
to be any trouble,
why do you walk into my dreams
every night?

Crossing

They say it was written on her heart.
Calais. The warm wind smells of urine.
The spire beyond the bay.
Queen over the water, you're in
another country, now only inches away.
Seagulls scream through the chalk face of the page,
into a foreign day.

Letter

a letter from you
on the morning doormat
unexpected
as a rainbow over Runcorn.

Domestic Interior

In the kitchen
she makes me a tree.
It tries to become a star
but fails.
It looks like a tree
trying to become a star.
It is made of cheese.

I eat it,
absentmindedly.

Outside,
the stars are turning into trees,
the trees are turning into cheese.

Love Story, Bosnia

(i.m. Bosko Brokić and Admira Ismić)

Bosko and Admira
huddle near in no-man's-land,
hand almost touching hand.
They do not move as other lovers.

Dead cellars of Sarajevo.
Birds beat on the empty wind
Playground silence broken
by the cackle of assault rifles.

The sweater his mother knitted for her
lies on the grave her mother cannot visit.

Helpless as words,
their few flowers wilt in the indifferent sun.

Yosemite

You are my Yosemite
all your deep declivities
– Schwarzwald, Colden Valley,
Col de Rousset –
and you are my Pacific
– the taste of sealrock and surf,
pinemist and clamshell –
the rounded slopes of childhood
– Moel Famau, Moel Maen Eva –
chapels riding their sides
in the Sion morning:
the blue remembered hills
– Wenlock Edge, Long Mynd,
The Wrekin –
that heave their forest fleece
into bedroom daylight.

The Cerise Swimsuit
(after William Carlos Williams)

so much depends
upon

a cerise swim
suit

hung out to
dry

in Laurel
Canyon

Thanksgiving

A storm,
its fur rubbed up the wrong way,
lowers over the heart of England,
like the memory of harsh words
waiting for the DON'T WALK sign.

The sun,
battling like Turner through the waves,
lifts the heart, the horizon,
like the warmth of a kiss
at the subway turnstile.

Some Other Guy

'Trick or treat'
behind the mask
I lurk in your street
hoping for kisses.

'A penny for the guy'
outside your gate
I lie, disguised,
wait for a smile.

You warm your hands
at someone else's bonfire;
rockets, Catherine-wheels explode
in someone else's garden.

Snowman

After I'd made a snowman
I used to cry with the pain;
not out in the cold, but by the fire
when my hands were warm again.

It's freezing here today;
sometimes it's just the same:
it's when we're warm together
I suddenly feel the pain.

Harvest Festival

Your new knickers
are patterned with fruit;
redcurrant and blackcurrant,
apple and blackberry,
ripe gooseberries,
tumble against black:
I bury my face
in their abundance,
the rich smell of autumn.
All good gifts around us …

We plough the fields and scatter

All safely gathered in,
we celebrate the harvest;
dark green leaves, orange-red fruit,
yellow flowers.

Thunderstorm, Nice

Lemons glow in the half-light;
Adam and Eve in the first rainstorm,
we hear the thunder,
see the shells of tortoises shine
like grapes washed on the vine;
the final tremors flicker between us,
last drops of rain on the oleander.

Oxford, Sunday, Rain

Sunday. Wet quadrangles,
the harsh angles of Gothic towers,
indifferent cobbles underfoot.
It is always like this, rain,
the bus from The High, sometimes
a taxi, this time the last time.
A face at the latticed window,
Bodleian treasures of memories.
Backpacked tourists huddle
in their anoraks. The train at Platform 2
is ten minutes late. It is always like this.
Sunday. Rain. The remembered taste.
A train. Dreaming choirs of birds
sing evensong in the evening garden
behind your room. 'I'll ring when I get back.
See you soon.' The train lurches late
through the growing gloom.

Rock Climber, Avon Gorge

I stand by your side
like Robert the Bruce
and watch him,
redtrousered,
try, try, try again
to scale the indifferent strata,
twinges of vertigo
through the soles of my feet
at the chasm
suspended
between us.

Spare the Face

refusing the blindfold
I watch you make the expected
daily
phonecall to him
head held high
gazing bravely into the gunbarrels.

Winter Garden

There is a garden in her face
Where roses and white lilies grow

The bathwater smelling of blackberries,
my hair of white nettles, my body
soaped with the scent of green ferns.

We walked in the Botanical Gardens
in winter. Small pink flowers
against the gloom. Berries bloomed,
cherry ripe. You rang, this morning.
There is a garden in this place,
of sorts. A lone honeysuckle
huddles against the frost, that rimes
the unchecked weeds of summer,
brown stalks of lily-of-the-valley.

O ruddier than the cherry,
O brighter than the berry

Tonight I meet you from the plane.
All I can offer, once again,
a winter garden,
the smell of blackberries, green ferns,
white nettles.

Mantelpiece

Between an Art Nouveau swirl
of yellow-green glass
and an embroidered heart
made by an unknown soldier
for his sweetheart
you clutch a paper cup of coffee
in gloved hands
brown velvet cap pulled low
shading the resentment.
A team deflates
the giant Snoopy behind you.
Thanksgiving. An invisible
N.Y.P.D. POLICE LINE DO NOT CROSS
between us.

On the landing, you are laughing,
your arms full of willowherb.

Love in Southport

By the marine lake
ducks, drakes, black-headed gulls
gobble crisps, squabble over discarded chips.
Pensioners peer in café windows, compare
the price of a cup of tea. Somewhere
over there, the sea. The little train
trundles along the Pier. 'Wish you were here'.
A male swan rises,

flaps his wings. Two more,
arse-upwards, white sails in the sunlight.
What will you be doing in N.Y.C. tonight?
Two painters paint the railings turquoise
and bright blue. Behind
the line of pines the sand whispers
your name. Nettles and bluebells.
Beyond, golfers push golfcarts towards senility.
Here, we trudge across the bridge
towards the unwelcoming sea.

Love in Blackpool

In a famous seaside place
that's noted for fresh air and not much else tonight
the lights from The Tower are lost in the fog
a lone dog patrols the shrouded beach
ghosts of pink, cheeky-bottomed girls
huge striped men who can't see their little Willy
haunt the deserted Pier
the Winter Gardens.
In every shuttered gift shop window
dusty sticks with horses-head handles
faded bars of rock
lettered all through say
I LOVE YOU. The bitter wind
has fish-and-chips on its breath.

Cemetery by the Sea

Bundled up like a child against the wind
that bends the stunted trees,
catches its salt breath between our lips,
bleaches drystone gorse to palest yellow,
that scours limewashed walls,
light blue window-frames,
the double-barrelled Norman church,
smashes the waves
against the island of forgotten saints –
you lean into the gale
like slate memorials of the dead,
upright, unforgettable, unforgotten.

Mother and Child

Wrapped in blue gingham he sits
rapt in contemplation of the mother,
she of him. Across the aisle
you are trapped between the poet's words
and the baby's smile, feel his warmth
across the black gingham lap,
the milky kiss, turn reluctantly
back to the page. Through the window,
behind the rushing landscape,
the old authentic angels sing.

Kiwi

I don't know about Lawrentian figs,
but for me it is messy and beautiful,
like eating ripe kiwifruit
without peeling them:
sweet succulence that stains the shirt,
lingers in the beard.

Reclining Female Nude

'Bocca Bacciata'
you are Titian, Tintoretto,
Corregio;
rose madder, pale sienna
pearled by morning light from the lagoon
in the Giorgione shadows.

Devon Morning

In this place
of sunshine and blown roses,
a turning sky,
where
I have not written you before
you write yourself
into the grass, tall nettles,
dragonflies,
your smile open
all the way to the river.

Coronary Care Unit

1

False dawn
of the desk lamp
night wind
from the electric fan
stirs the leaves in the partition curtains.
In the real, striped, green dawn
they bring back cups of tea
from the water-hole
as we watch from the sheeted savannah.

2

'Cardiac arrest in the coronary care unit'
the life next door
flickers beyond the frail curtain.
He asks for his singlet. They've never heard
the word. 'Cardiac arrest …'
Don't they know
he means a vest?

3

Lungs strain towards the light.
Jagged lines on the monitor. Electric bleeps.
Breath distant as sunlit, sheep-filled hills.
Outside, the terraces, the tower-blocks
cough black night.

4

The hollow roar of his chest
dominates the room
like the skyline outside.
His last sharp cries
wheel in the air like seagulls.

5

As I reach out, snatch at sleep
sometimes it seems I catch your hand.
Or at the end, far along the breathless road
you stand, arms full of flowers
beside a wood in Normandy,
mouth open with delight at the sight
of long green leaves, purple blossom.
Along the gulping hours, moments torn,
your face. Your voice, joining sleepy
in The Lobster Quadrille. Our love
a yellow filament that runs across the screen
above my bed.

HOME AND AWAY

The Entry of Christ into Liverpool in 1964, 1962–64

Père Ubu in Liverpool, 1962

Bird Dying for its Country, 1963–64

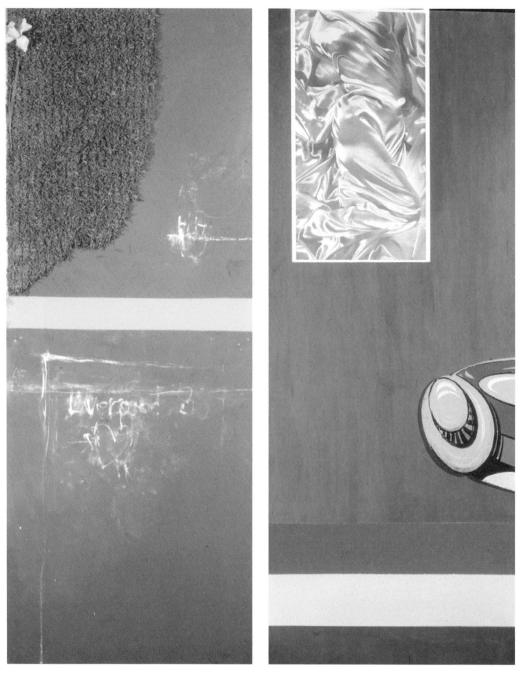

Liverpool 8 Four Seasons Painting, 1964; *Spring* [*left*], *Summer* [*right*]

Liverpool 8 Four Seasons Painting, 1964; Autumn [*left*], Winter [*right*]

The Day of the Dead, Hope Street, 1998

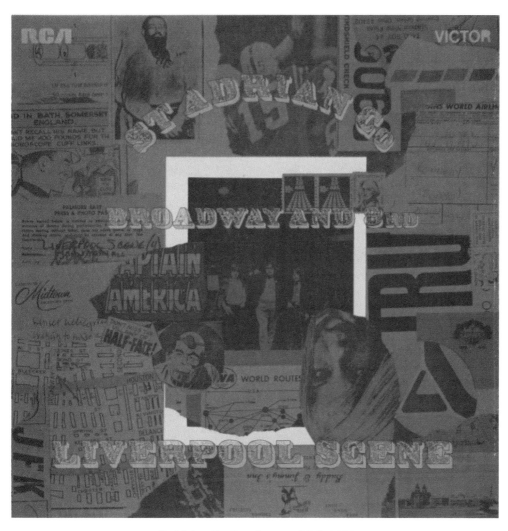

St Adrian Co, Broadway and 3rd, 1970

Giverny I, 1988

Graveyard, The Parsonage, Haworth, 1994

El Khazneh, Petra, 1993

Thanksgiving Day Parade, New York City III, 1995

Umfolozi, 1999–2000

Metropolis

'If I'd have known I was living in one of the most exciting periods of recent history, I'd have taken more notice.' This was a typical Henri witticism, but in fact, Adrian was very much aware of the times in which he lived, as well as the place, and if anybody had a paint-stained finger on the pulse of the sixties' Zeitgeist it was him. But although revelling in the period, and celebrating it in his work, his poems are often imbued with a sense of nostalgia. The longing for an imagined perfect childhood, the ideal lover, always just out of reach. The Adrian I knew was not a tortured soul, for he considered himself a lucky man to have earned a living as a poet and an artist, but what gives his poems their distinctive character is not only the painter's eye and the jazz enthusiast's ear, but the feeling that when he wrote 'Don't worry, everything's going to be all right' he didn't really believe it.

Roger McGough
London, 2007

The Entry of Christ into Liverpool

City morning. dandelionseeds   blowing from wasteground.
smell of overgrown privethedges. children's voices
in the distance. sounds from the river.
round the corner into Myrtle St. Saturdaymorning shoppers
headscarves. shoppingbaskets. dogs.

then
    down the hill

THE SOUND OF TRUMPETS
cheering and shouting in the distance
children running
icecream vans
flags breaking out over buildings
black and red green and yellow
Union Jacks   Red Ensigns
LONG LIVE SOCIALISM
stretched against the blue sky
over St George's hall

Now the procession

THE MARCHING DRUMS
hideous masked Breughel faces of old ladies in the crowd
yellow masks of girls in curlers and headscarves
smelling of factories
Masks   Masks   Masks
red masks   purple masks   pink masks

crushing surging carrying me along
down the hill past the Philharmonic The Labour Exchange
excited feet crushing the geraniums in St Luke's Gardens
placards   banners   posters
Keep Britain White

End the War in Vietnam
God Bless Our Pope
Billboards hoardings drawings on pavements
words painted on the road
STOP GO HALT
the sounds of pipes and drums down the street
little girls in yellow and orange dresses paper flowers
embroidered banners
Loyal Sons of King William Lodge, Bootle
Masks more Masks crowding in off buses
standing on walls climbing fences

familiar faces among the crowd
faces of my friends the shades of Pierre Bonnard and
Guillaume Apollinaire
Jarry cycling carefully through the crowd. A black cat
picking her way underfoot
posters
signs
gleaming salads
COLMAN'S MUSTARD
J. Ensor, Fabriqueur de Masques
HAIL JESUS, KING OF THE JEWS
straining forward to catch a glimpse through the crowd,
red hair   white robe   grey donkey
familiar face
trafficlights zebracrossings
GUIN
GUINN
GUINNESS IS
white bird dying unnoticed in a corner
splattered feathers
blood running merged with the neonsigns
in a puddle
GUINNESS   IS   GOOD
GUINNESS   IS   GOOD   FOR

Masks   Masks   Masks   Masks   Masks
GUINNESS IS GOOD FOR YOU

brassbands cheering loudspeakers blaring
clatter of police horses
ALL POWER TO THE CONSTITUENT
ASSEMBLY
masks cheering glittering teeth
daffodils trodden underfoot

BUTCHERS OF JERUSALEM
banners cheering drunks stumbling and singing
masks
masks
masks

evening
thin sickle moon
pale blue sky
flecked with bright orange clouds
streamers newspapers discarded paper hats
blown slowly back up the hill by the evening wind
dustmen with big brooms sweeping the gutters
last of the crowds waiting at bus-stops
giggling schoolgirls quiet businessmen
me
walking home
empty chip-papers drifting round my feet.

Liverpool Poems

1

GO TO WORK ON A BRAQUE!

2

Youths disguised as stockbrokers
Sitting on the grass eating the Sacred Mushroom.

3

Liverpool I love your horny-handed tons of soil.

4

PRAYER FROM A PAINTER TO ALL CAPITALISTS:

Open your wallets and repeat after me
'HELP YOURSELF!'

5

There's one way of being sure of keeping fresh
LIFEBUOY helps you rise again on the 3rd day
after smelling something that smelt like other people's socks.

6

Note for a definition of optimism:
A man trying the door of Yates Wine Lodge
At quarter past four in the afternoon.

7

I have seen Père UBU walking across Lime St
And Alfred Jarry cycling down Elliott Street.

8

And I saw DEATH in Upper Duke St
Cloak flapping black tall Batman collar
Striding tall shoulders down the hill past the Cathedral
    brown shoes slightly down at the heel.

9

Unfrocked Chinese mandarins holding lonely feasts in
Falkner Sq gardens to enjoy the snow

10

Prostitutes in the snow in Canning St like strange erotic snowmen
And Marcel Proust in the Kardomah eating Madeleine butties dipped in tea.

11

Wyatt James Virgil and Morgan Earp with Doc Holliday
Shooting it out with the Liver Birds at the Pier Head.

12

And a Polish gunman young beautiful dark glasses
combatjacket/staggers down Little St Bride St blood
dripping moaning clutches/collapses down a back jigger
coughing/falls in a wilderness of Dazwhite washing.

Mrs Albion, You've Got a Lovely Daughter

(for Allen Ginsberg)

Albion's most lovely daughter sat on the banks of the Mersey
    dangling her landing stage in the water.

The daughters of Albion
    arriving by underground at Central Station
    eating hot ecclescakes at the Pierhead
    writing 'Billy Blake is Fab' on a wall in Mathew Street

    taking off their navyblue schooldrawers and
    putting on nylon panties ready for the night

The daughters of Albion
    see the moonlight beating down on them in Bebington
    throw away their chewinggum ready for the goodnight kiss
sleep in the dinnertime sunlight with old men
    looking up their skirts in St Johns Gardens
comb their darkblonde hair in suburban bedrooms
powder their delicate little nipples/wondering if tonight will
    be the night
their bodies pressed into dresses or sweaters
lavender at The Cavern or pink at The Sink

The daughters of Albion wondering how to explain why they
    didn't go home

The daughters of Albion
    taking the dawn ferry to tomorrow
    worrying about what happened
    worrying about what hasn't happened
    lacing up blue sneakers over brown ankles
    fastening up brown stockings to blue suspenderbelts

Beautiful boys with bright red guitars
in the spaces between the stars

Reelin' an' a-rockin'
Wishin' an' a-hopin'
Kissin' an' a-prayin'
Lovin' an' a-layin'

Mrs Albion, you've got a lovely daughter.

Death of a Bird in the City II

(for Philip Jones Griffiths and his photographs)

Guns are bombarding Piccadilly
Firing at ten million splattered white dying birds

Doors thrown open
Girls mouths screaming
The last unbearable white bird
Spotlit, slowly struggling threshing against blackness
Crucified on the easel
SCHWEPPES
GUINNESS IS …
The lights are going out …
A blind old woman with light running from her glasses
Seeing nothing.
The plaster Christ has got up and is kneeling before the plaster donkey

Buildings are falling silently
Neonsigns are running like blood
The COCA-COLA sun is setting
The plaster Mary following the star
B.P.   MAX FACTOR
To where the Three Kings lay
The last bird has leapt weeping
Onto the neon wheel
Delicious
REFRESHING
Screaming through the echoing ruins of Piccadilly
Under the bombardment of the night.

Piccadilly Poems

1

Piccadilly
Vast overflowing abundances of poemness
LEWIS'S
… THE NATIONAL BANK
A bus 83a O God in my mind screaming
dragged beneath the wheels
Horatory
Minatory
Messianic
the ghost of Guillaume Apollinaire
watches from glass and concrete perspectives of bus stations.

2

DAFFODILS ARE NOT REAL!

3

Sitting in a city square in the April sunshine
I see the first beachheads of the Martian invasion
Lapping over the rusticated walls.

4

7 cowboys stride into the city
Hitch their horses to a bus terminal
Sun on their shirts sweat on their faces dust caking their jeans
Gun resting easily on hip.

5

NIGHT the time of the terrible neon wheel.

6

The smell of grass being mowed in the square;
I sit in a café in Piccadilly
And think of Yves Tanguy
Alone in the crowded dugout eating sandwiches full of spiders.

Welcome to My World

'Don't find me'
snarl the poems
from the headlines
    'Ne me trouvez
pas' cry
the objects
from the beaches.

I Want to Paint

Part One

I want to paint
2000 dead birds crucified on a background of night
Thoughts that lie too deep for tears
Thoughts that lie too deep for queers
Thoughts that move at 186,000 miles / second
The Entry of Christ into Liverpool in 1966
The Installation of Roger McGough to the Chair of Poetry at Oxford
Francis Bacon making the President's Speech at the Royal Academy Dinner

I want to paint
50 life-sized nudes of Marianne Faithfull
(all of them painted from life)
Welsh Maids by Welsh Waterfalls
Heather Holden as Our Lady of Haslingden
A painting as big as Piccadilly full of neon signs buses
Christmas decorations and beautiful girls with dark blonde hair shading their
     faces

I want to paint
The assassination of the entire Royal Family
Enormous pictures of every pavingstone in Canning Street
The Beatles composing a new National Anthem
Brian Patten writing poems with a flamethrower on disused ferryboats
A new cathedral 50 miles high made entirely of pramwheels
An empty Woodbine packet covered in kisses
I want to paint
A picture made from the tears of dirty-faced children in Chatham Street

I want to paint
I LOVE YOU across the steps of St George's Hall

I want to paint
        pictures.

Part Two

I want to paint
The Simultaneous and Historical Faces of Death
10,000 shocking pink hearts with your name on
The phantom negro postmen who bring me money in my dreams
The first plastic daffodil of spring pushing its way
through the OMO packets in the Supermarket
The portrait of every 6th-form schoolgirl in the country
A full-scale map of the world with YOU at the centre
An enormous lily-of-the-valley with every flower on a separate canvas

Lifesize jellybabies shaped like Hayley Mills
A black-and-red flag flying over Parliament
I want to paint
Every car crash on all the motorways of England
Père Ubu drunk at 11 o'clock at night in Lime Street
A SYSTEMATIC DERANGEMENT OF ALL THE SENSES
in black running letters 50 miles high over Liverpool
I want to paint
Pictures that children can play hopscotch on
Pictures that can be used as evidence at murder trials
Pictures that can be used to advertise cornflakes
Pictures that can be used to frighten naughty children
Pictures worth their weight in money
Pictures that tramps can live in
Pictures that children would find in their stockings on Christmas morning
Pictures that teenage lovers can send each other
I want to paint
        pictures.

Bomb Commercials

(for two voices)

1 A. Get PAD nuclear meat for humans
     B. Don't give your family ordinary meat, give them PAD
     A. P.A.D. –Prolongs Active Death
     B. Enriched with nourishing marrowbone strontium.

2 A. All over the world, more and more people are changing to
BOMB

     B. BOMB – The international passport to smoking ruins

3 B. *… so then I said 'well let's all go for a picnic and we went and it was all right except for a bit of sand in the butties and then of course the wasps and Michael fell in the river but what I say is you can't have everything perfect can you so just then there was a big bang and the whole place caught fire and something happened to Michael's arm and I don't know what happened to my Hubby and it's perhaps as well as there were only four pieces of Kit-Kat so we had one each and then we had to walk home 'cos there weren't any buses…'*
     A. HAVE A BREAK – HAVE A KIT-KAT

4 A. Everyday in cities all over England people are breathing in Fall-out
     B. Get the taste of the Bomb out of your mouth with OVAL FRUITS

5 A. General Howard J. Sherman has just pressed the button that killed 200 million people. A BIG job with BIG responsibilities. The General has to decide between peace and the extinction of the human race …
     B. But he can't tell Stork from Butter.

Summer Poems Without Words

(To be distributed in leaflet form to the audience. Each poem should be tried within the next seven days.)

1 Try to imagine your next hangover

2 Travel on the Woodside ferry with your eyes closed. Travel back with them open.

3 Look for a black cat. Stroke it. This will be either lucky or unlucky.

4 Find a plastic flower. Hold it up to the light.

5 Next time you see someone mowing a lawn smell the smell of freshly cut grass.

6 Watch *Coronation Street*. Listen to the 'B' side of the latest Dusty Springfield record.

7 Sit in a city square in the sunlight. Remember the first time you made love.

8 Look at every poster you pass next time you're on a bus.

9 Open the *News of the World* at page 3. Read between the lines.

10 The next time you clean your teeth *think* about what you're doing.

The New 'Our Times'

(for Félix Fénéon)

1

At 3 p.m. yesterday, a Mr Adolphus Edwards, a Jamaican immigrant, was pecked to death by a large Bronze Eagle in Upper Parliament St. A US State Dept spokesman said later, 'We have no comment to make as of this time.'

2

Police-Constable George Williams, who was partially blinded by a 15lb jellybaby thrown at a passing pop singer, is to be retired on half-pension.

3

Bearded Liverpool couple put out of misery in night by drip oil heater, court told.

4

A certain Mrs Elspeth Clout, of Huyton, was killed by an unidentified falling object. It was thought to be a particularly hard stool evacuated from the toilet of a passing aeroplane.

5

2 chip-shop proprietors were today accused of selling human ears fried in batter. One of them said: 'We believe there is room for innovation in the trade.'

6

Fatality in Kardomah bomb outrage: Waitress buried Alive under two thousand Danish pastries.

7

At the inquest on Paul McCartney, aged 21, described as a popular singer and guitarist, P.C. Smith said, in evidence, that he saw one of the accused, Miss Jones, standing waving bloodstained hands shouting 'I got a bit of his liver'.

The New, Fast, Automatic Daffodils

(New variation on Wordsworth's 'Daffodils')

I wandered lonely as
THE NEW, FAST DAFFODIL
    FULLY AUTOMATIC
that floats on high o'er vales and hills
The Daffodil is generously dimensioned to accommodate four adult passengers
10,000 saw I at a glance
Nodding their new anatomically shaped heads in sprightly dance
Beside the lake beneath the trees
    in three bright modern colours
red, blue and pigskin
The Daffodil de luxe is equipped with a host of useful accessories
including windscreen wiper and washer with joint control
A Daffodil doubles the enjoyment of touring at home or abroad

in vacant or in pensive mood
SPECIFICATION:
    Overall width   1.44 m (57")
    Overall height   1.38m (54.3")
    Max. speed   105 km/hr (65 m.p.h.)
       (also cruising speed)
DAFFODIL
    RELIABLE – ECONOMICAL
DAFFODIL
    THE BLISS OF SOLITUDE
DAFFODIL
    The Variomatic Inward Eye
Travelling by Daffodil you can relax and enjoy every mile of the journey.

(Cut-up of Wordsworth's poem plus Dutch motor-car leaflet)

On the Late Late Massachers Stillbirths and Deformed Children a Smoother Lovelier Skin Job

The seven-day beauty plan:
Avenge O Lord thy slaughter'd saints, whose bones
Will cause up to 1 million deaths from leukaemia
Forget not, in thy book record their groans
Now for the vitally important step. Cream your face and neck a second time
No American president world-famous for beauty creams
responsible for the freedom and safety of so many young offenders
TODAY'S MEN OF ACTION
The Triple Tyrant Macmillan Kennedy Watkinson
The West governments are satisfied as to the moral necessity to resume Racing
     from Newmarket
EXTRA SPECIAL!
Atmospheric testing: A test card is shown
continuously from 10 a.m. until 15 minutes
before slayn by the bloody Piemontese
why pay higher fares?
There is always trouble when President Kennedy the jovial gravel-voiced little
     sailor
defends glamorous Olive Oyl from contamination of the atmosphere
EXTRA MONEY their moans
The Vales redoubled to the Hills
Another fire blazes in the city of London AND ALL THAT JAZZ
Do you draw your curtains with a walking-stick?
The mutation was caused by a heavy dose of radiation received
by the Mother at Hiroshima
This baby's eyes and nose had merged into
one misshapen feature in the middle of its
forehead lost 6" from Hips
sufferers can now wear fashion stockings
Early may fly the Babylonian who
followed by

TOMORROW'S WEATHER
The Epilogue
close down.

Cut-up of John Milton's Sonnet XV, 'On the late Massacher in Piemont' / TV Times / CND leaflet.

The Dance of Death

autumn to winter:
willowherb turns indigo
against the orange of its going
bonfires in backyards
hold the fitful dusk at bay
flushed children's faces
candles in pumpkins
strains of the 'Dies Irae' heard in the distance.

Dancing figures against the fading skyline
bony feet through withered leaves
leaping singing flapping like stormclouds
Death the Magician
conjuring darkness out of daylight
Death and the Lovers
crouching behind the settee peering through the curtains
Death and the Maiden
cold phalanxes of fingers over goosepimpled flesh
probing the warm and secret places
' ... there will now follow a party political broadcast
on behalf of Death ... this programme will be shown
on all channels ... '
Death the Politician
polished white face carefully sipping water
adjusting his fireside manner
DEATH RULES OK
scrawlcd on a wall outside the football stadium
Death the Terrorist Death the Avenger
O there is no hiding from the secret bomber
the parcel left unnoticed in the crowded discothèque
Death the Trafficwarden Death the Controller
bodies spilling everywhere
trainsmash or planecrash

carbrakes on tarmac
Death and the Soldier
familiar companion
riding a troop-carrier in camouflage gravecloths
Death and the Boatman
steering the October ferry to Eridanus
Death the Popsinger –
obscene spangled bony limbs gyrating –
Death and the Drunkard
grinning behind the barmaid's smile
Death and the Junkie
kindly refilling the hypodermic
Death and the Priest
mocking laughter from behind the altar
sly white face behind the confessional
Death and the Schoolgirl
cold hand up her gymslip in the autumn park
Death and the Farmer
following the furrow seed falling barren
Death in the Supermarket,
Corner-shop, Greengrocers',
Dance-hall and Waiting-room,
Alehouse and News-stand,
Housewife and Bunnygirl
join in the sarabande
hold hands and dance, dance
as the lightnings whirl
dance, dance, dance to the darkness …

eve,
and the Michaelmas moon
rise in the firtrees
last strains of music
heard from the deadlands
November dreams
lost amongst stormclouds.

Metropolis

(for David Gascoyne)

1

gravelponds along long lines
fruit-trees heavy in the autumn sunlight
disturbed only by the falling brickdust
and the distant roar of engines in the morning air.

blackberries glinting in the sunlight
poised against the sky   toppling into enormous pits
hayfields   troutstreams   drystone walls
falling   tumbling   rolling before the gleaming blades
squashed hedgehogs dying owls rabbits screaming
grass and tiny bodies tangled in the clay
before the march of giant earthmovers.

o stars trees ponds
tornup roots of farmhouses
gape into the mist
allnight roar of a thousand cementmixers
acetylene lights flooding the sky.

2

apocalypse of weirs foaming into polluted canals
endless landscape of factoryfields
chimneys belching dark into the distance
all roads home gleaming far away silver seen briefly through the drifting clouds.
vast reactors megatheriums of pylons
tangled webs of cables blotting out the light
save for bright sodium-lights above the rushing expressways
flyover   cloverleaf   underpass
one way only   every which way
roadways layered up into the darkness.

3

concrete empty electric hallways
echoing with the sound of Muzak
shopfronts still boarded   shuttering still on the pillars
scaffolding everywhere through the haze
glass towers into the sky
acres of polished tables   boardroom carpet
empty halls of computers and filing cabinets.

endless escalators   vistas of plump thighs
nylon curved crammed tight with bursting flesh
tight glimpsed whitecotton secrets
soft female smell in the secret darkness
nerveless fingers immobile on trains
touching the warm imagined places
vistas of pink nipples haloed through delicate lace
disappearing out of the corners of the eyes.

NIGHT   the neon landscape
the soft purr of skysigns switching on at evening
like the roosting of longdead pigeons
nightlong litany of hammers and rockdrills
green light flickering from the wall-to-wall telescreens.

4

huge bridges   majestic arches
spanning the longdead beds of rivers
dried pramwheels   rusty cans   bones of dead animals
stagnant pools rainbowed with oil
where fishes once swarmed.

limitless vistas of bungalows and tower-flats
behind the highways
obscured constantly by the gathering darkness
ceaseless flashing of commutercars under the yellow lights

gaping mouths of endless tunnels
gleaming silver trains swish and rattle into blackness
old videotapes of trees played rushingly past the empty windows
stereo birdsong through the airconditioned silence.

The Triumph of Death

'Thunder in the dark at Adrian Henri's...'

1

birdsong
dropping into space between the sodium-lights
footsteps echo on the wet yellow pavement
down the hill lights of the unknown hometown
bright across the river

First faint chords drift in from the orchestra
woodwinds high in the air
light from the evening sun catching the river
dockyards at the end of the street
flicker with the first smudges of flame

sudden skull-head peering from round the street-corner
seen for a moment from the top of the street
shopping-bag in hand
white beckoning skeleton hand unnoticed behind the parked cars
darkling sky clouding the silver water

2

Fanfare of French Horns:
cars pile relentless into each other at trafficlights
grinning skeletal policemen
ride ambulances over pedestrians
klaxon-horns blaring

MUSIC FULL UP:
strings brass timpani
hoarse screams of owls from parks
despairing wail of sirens from sinking ferryboats
roar of exploding oil-tanks

walls of flame round abandoned tankers
figures of men broken on wheels against the lurid sky

high
above
squadron upon squadron
of dark figures
wheel triumphantly
row derisively amongst the carnage
salmon leap despairingly from the boiling waters

3

images from the haunted screen:

in the deserted cinema
a trapped usherette
smashes shattering the waxen mask
grinning hideous face beneath
football-crowds melting like waxworks
faces running marble eyeballs fallen from sockets
rooftops at crazy angles
dark figure in at the bedroom window
classrooms burst into flame
a skeleton exposes his rotting pelvis
to the helpless gaze of a class of schoolgirls

4

typists   shopgirls   errandboys
scream hopelessly
run towards ornamental gardens
from the falling buildings
white mocking figures insolently riding the debris
neat gardens in St James's Cemetery
torn apart
wreathed and cellophaned flowers tumbled aside

as gravecloths burst into the light
white blinking stumbling figures
queue at the gravemouths

black crows perch on the remains of department stores
dying seagulls splattered helpless against the sky
vultures wait on the Cathedral tower
busloads of darkrobed skeleton figures
raping laughing dancing singing
a revolving door spins unheeded
the hotel lounge littered with corpses

gibbets long as vermin-poles down the middle of streets
mocking roar of music behind the explosions
thunder in the dark
light only from the burning earth
dark   dark   dark
white bony mocking faces everywhere

5

And you beside me, my morning girl of the shadows
the inscrutable nurse always at the morning bedside
white breasts sprouting naked beneath your black cloak
head thrown back swirls of rivermist in your hair
take me fold me forever in your warm darkness
suck the cold life from my willing veins
lost in the final dark embrace

black barge straining waiting at the riverbank.

Death in the Suburbs

The end of the world will surely come
in Bromley South or Opington

morning in the suburbs:
sunlight thrown like a blanket
over pink-and-white vistas
villas detached and undetached
islanded with flowering cherry,
stone ravens guard the gateposts
the roof left unguarded,
each man's garden a province unto itself
linked only by birdsong
and the tasteful cooing of doves in hedges
magnolia-petals on deep lawns
little clouds of white and purple round rockeries
frozen veils of appleblossom round every doorway.

the earth
moves
sudden
tiny snowstorms of cherryblossom
a black cat runs apprehensive
flocks of starlings
startle from bushes
slow-growing crescendo
of crashing picture-windows
gardens
uprooted
blown   pinkandwhite   skyhigh
frozen agonies of begonias
held for a moment like a blurred polaroid
lawns flung like carpets
golfclubs   potting-sheds   wheeled shopping-baskets
hurled into orbit

deepfreezes burst open
prepackaged meals spilling everywhere
invitations to whist-drives   coffee-mornings
letters to long-haired sons at campus universities
never to be delivered
pinboards   posters of Che Guevara   stereo systems
continental quilts   rows of neat lettuces
blameless chihuahuas   au pair girls
still wet from dreams of Italian waiters
mothers-in-law   bullfight trophies   sensible wooden toys
whirled helpless in a vortex
rockeries like asteroids
blizzards of appleblossom
against the April sunlight

villa after villa
flickers off like television
birdsounds
blur into the silence
like a vacuum
heaps of white entrails
nestling amid lilies-of-the-valley
ripple like tarmac
gravel chatters   the crazy dance of pavingstones
whole avenues implode
gantries and railway bridges
quiet sidings
engulfed by avalanches of privet and hawthorn
waves of chalk earth flecked with hemlock- and nettle-roots
burying commuter-stations.

faraway,
the first distant ripples
flutter dovecots
disturb the pigeons
roosting in oasthouses

weekend cottages
doff their thatch to the sky
mountaintops tumble like cumuli
gales of earth
ravage through ryefields
pylons tremble like seismographs
cries of children
circling like seagulls
echo the distance

a
solitary
picnicker
sitting on a breakwater
above the red, flint-strewn beach
hears the distant thunder
as clifftops crumble
looks up from the light scumbling the silver water
to see the horizon catch fire
showers of small stones
smell of uprooted samphire
the last slice of ham   a packet of biscuits   the small black notebook
slip away unseen
as the concrete rears vertical
his ears' last echo
the cries of lost sea-birds
one drifting pink petal
catches the dying sunlight.

Wasteland

1
gaunt canals
wet cathedrals   soggy boulevards
leading to no fixed abode
ill winds
blowing from nowhere to nowhere
cracked bells   calling none to worship
stirring dead leaves
round rotting treestumps
… heaps of broken images … wet paper
bikewheels   gas-stoves   dead christmas trees
… lips that would kiss …
pink uprooted sandstone
gleam through the mist
haze of blazing rafters   rooftrees
… eyes not in dreams …
whitewashed walls fall silently
telegraph wires slung pole to pole
across the wasteland

Lady of the Estuary
mudflats   rubbishdumps
… falling falling …
drowned in the sound of distant traffic
my uncompleted graffiti
sprayed on your walls
grey suburbs on a grey day
lead me away from you
echoes of ghostly children's laughter
from forgotten hopscotch pavements.

2

Business is brisk here at the wasteland.
Cars cross the crisscross roads
taking shortcuts to nowhere.
At the coast – they tell us – the seas are rising.

My girlfriend is 21 and says she is doomed
she works in a bar in Rats' Alley
where the dead men snatch handbags.

In the bar,
a skull with a burning cigarette demands her attention
the clock in everyone's face
has stopped.
The face I see in the mirror
is not mine. I drink up and leave.

The pall of smoke grows thicker across the wasteland.
The weather report says 'unsettled'.
Broken glass like a kingfisher in the sunset.
She will walk home alone, uneasy figures in the darkness.

O dream in vain of roses and butterflies,
the door in the forest,
the dark somnambulist waits at the window.

3

Cruellest Month

We make plans to go away for Easter.
Dream of wet lambs staggering into the Shropshire air
the deep, violet-haunted hedges of Devon
the white cliffs of Normandy, red-stained as the backs of Courbet cattle.

Then
decide instead to holiday at home
stock up with decent wines, provisions
loins of pork, legs of veal
broccoli, endives and tomatoes
jostle the refrigerator
the deep-freeze hums its satisfaction.

We settle down,
plan ahead with the TV papers,
the room filled with the petticoat-smell of daffodils.

Outside,
the nightmares howl across the wasteland.

4

The Blues in Rats' Alley

I think we're in Rats' Alley where the dead men lost their bones
Think we're in Rats' Alley where the dead men lost their bones
Where the vandals smashed the windows and they took the telephones.

Tell me, Mrs Porter, what you done to me?
Tell me, Mrs Porter, what you done to me?
Took away your daughter, left me here in misery.

Standing in Rats' Alley where the cats won't walk at night
Yes, I'm standing in Rats' Alley where the cats won't go at night
Try to speak your name but you're always out of sight.

Standing on the platform waiting for the train
On the empty platform, trying to see the train
Never heard that whistle, now I'm here in Rats' Alley again.

Take me back, baby, it's you I hate to lose
Hurry back, baby, we don't have time to choose
Take me from this wasteland, don't leave me with these Rats' Alley Blues.

5

(for André Breton)

these
waste
lands
vague terrains

                                        and the moon

where I wander
indecipherable statues
old boxing-gloves
lonely as
shards of shattered saucers

                                        and the shadow

from the dance floor
a host   a cloud
of
roots that clutch
stirred by
ill winds   lost laughter
down
fall
of the evening lands
blowing from
nowhere
to nowhere.

Adrian Henri's Talking Toxteth Blues

Well, I woke up this morning, there was buzzing overhead
Saw the helicopter as I got out of my bed,
Smelt the smell of burning, saw the buildings fall,
Bulldozers pulling down next door's wall.
    Toxteth nightmare …
          … yes …
            … city with a hangover.

Then I remembered what happened last night
The sirens and the shouting and the TV lights,
Banging on the riotshields, petrol bombs in flames,
Cars all ablazing, shattered window-frames.
    Felt sick to my stomach …
          … don't cry for me …
           … Upper Parly.

Saw a busy lying blood pouring from his head,
Saw one stop a paving stone, thought that he was dead.
Heard the sound of engines in the bright orange night,
Saw the headlights blazing, saw the crowd in flight.
    One of them …
          … didn't run fast enough …
        … Land Rovers …
          … long way from the farm.

Well, I saw the Chief Constable up on TV
And the Superintendents, but they never saw me,
Saw the Home Secretary and the Minister for Riots,
And all them social workers who just never keep quiet.
      … never met a one of them …
        … neither did the coppers.

Saw a woman walking in the firelight's glare,
'Hey, Aunty Maggy, what you doing there?'
Arms full of liquor and a portable TV,
Said, 'All the rest are doing it, why not me?
    … do yourself a favour, son,
      … nice music centre …
        … just over there.'

Well, I thought a bit about it and I took her advice
Crowd was having fun and the goods looked nice,
Then a scuffer copped me and they threw me in a van,
Took me off to Risley and the Magistrate Man.
    … exemplary sentence …
      … act as a deterrent …
        … law'n'order …
         … Toxteth nightmare …
          … city …
          … with a
            hangover.

Liverpool Poems

1

White
under the orange lights
a rabbit
lopes along Hope St.
at 3 a.m.

2

a Hardman St. wino
demands money from a man
getting out of a van
marked WAR ON WANT.

3

'If I cannot do great things
I will do small things in a great way'
the kitten on the poster says
above her neat grey head
as she signs the death-certificate.

4

a plump young pigeon
dying in Rodney St.
whistles as ineffectually
as the tramp with the penny whistle on the corner.

5

in St. Luke's gardens a drunk rises from a urine-splashed bench
lurches across the neat grass with total concentration
to pick an orange geranium.

6

the last throes of summer
reflected blinding from the river
at the foot of the hill
the first hint of October
stirs poems along the cobbled street.

Suburban Landscape with Figures

Dusk. A suburban street. The smell
of lilacs. A man is walking
a small black-and-white dog.
At the corner it pauses, lifts a leg
against a fence, turns and focuses
its one good eye on the beloved master.
He pats it, absentmindedly.

Forced to see his grandfather's flesh
startled alive to his touch,
keeping him there in your head for ever;
all the nice young men,
the powdered bodies
propped carefully in armchairs,
placed carefully beneath floorboards,
long conversations in front of the telly
that never need a reply.

'They are not dead
but only sleeping'

Dusk. A suburban street. The smell
of lilacs. A man is walking
a small black-and-white dog.
At the corner it pauses, lifts a leg
against a fence, turns and focuses
its one good eye on the beloved master.
He pats it, absentmindedly.
In the flat he has just left, a pan
simmers on the gas-stove. In it,
a young man's severed head,
eyes incurious, bobs and bubbles.

Outside, shadows gather in the lilacs,
the buddleias.

Shadowland

This is Shadowland,
a place where nothing is as it seems:
a place of voices, faces from your dreams.
Who casts this shadow? What's behind that door?
What does the Weather Forecast have in store?
What lurks behind the Banham locks?
Who's that sleeping in a cardboard box?
What can you see through the double glazing?
Who's that gazing vacantly at the sky?

Government restrictions, unfortunately,
don't allow us to ask how or why.

In the interests of balance, of course, we have to say
that everything on the economic front
is great. The indicators indicate
an upward trend. What? You lost it all?
Don't worry, friend. It's just a blip,
a few percentage points. Everything points
to an upsurge. The F.T. 100, The Dow Jones,
bring words of hope and joy
through cordless telephones.

So step into this twilight world,
knock on any door. We're sure
you'll find it interesting.
Don't worry if the one you've picked
seems to be derelict. Call it
'Ripe for Improvement'. The whole movement's
towards conservation. Generous grants available.
It's all saleable; a whole nation for sale
with only history to offer; it's all the rage:

just dress it up and call it
Heritage.

Welcome to Shadowland!

It's the
GRAND BARGAIN
NEVER-TO-BE-REPEATED
DEEP-CUT ROCK-BOTTOM
SUPERSALE OF THE CENTURY!
Television, Radio,
everything must go!
Hospitals and science-labs,
everything's up for grabs,
even the water that you drink,
in fact, anything you can think of.
We're getting stronger: fresh air?
You won't get that for free much longer.
Don't worry if you find the payments hard.
No problem. Just use
your credit card.

Voices. Voices from a dream. Voices that seem
as real as the person next to you on the bus.
Who's speaking? Them? You? Us?

They lived next door for thirty years. *Years.*
By the time we heard the ambulance it was
too late. *Too late.* Anyway you don't like
to be nosy. *Nosy.* Not like some. *Some.*
Hanging over the gate to see. *See.* Catch me.
Catch me. Of course, we've always said 'Hello'.
'Hello'. A card through the letterbox at Christmas.
Christmas. How were we to know …

Waiting for Peter in Leicester Square. Why
isn't he there? Will Tinkerbell magic us away?
Will Mr. and Mrs. Darling say
'Come in lads, make yourselves at home'?
Home. A magic place as distant as
the Empire State. It's getting late.
The neon signs blink on in Never-Never Land.

Fed and changed like a babby.
Look at me. Neither use nor ornament.
Like a broken vase pushed to the back
of a shelf. An embarrassment to them,
and myself. They'll be better off when I go.
Go where? The minutes, the seconds start.
So slow …

No marks out of ten, again.
The black marks pile up like shadows
on a winter afternoon. Soon they'll be back
asking questions I don't know how
to answer. Questions pile up
like fallen leaves. *You could be out there now,*
kicking through them under the streetlights.
Shadows lengthen like question-marks
in the empty classroom.

'Rockabye baby on the tenth floor
Mummy will hold you nice and secure
When Mummy breaks the cradle will fall
Down will come baby, Mummy and all'

Voices. Voices from a dream …

She stands, proud as Britannia,
rules the way we judge, and are judged.

She weighs us in her cold scales;
her ways mysterious, we do not see
what she weighs against us.
They say she's blind; I'm sure that's true;
be thankful: one of these days
she might turn her stony gaze
on you.

This is Shadowland. Is it just a nightmare?
Is it real? What are we supposed to feel?
And what are we supposed to do?
A twilight place where your worst dreams come true.
Frightened? Desperate? Confused?
Don't worry: it couldn't happen
to you.

Morning, Liverpool 8

In Blackburne Place and Canning Street
the terraces half-wake,
stretch their balconies;
cast-iron railings, Ionic columns
blink into daylight from
a nightmare of bulldozers,
dripping water, charred beams,
distant dreams of hopscotch,
hoofbeats on cobblestones. The mirror tells
of a bright new face, does not reflect
the past neglect. Hope Place
and Huskisson tell of the nightmare
almost gone.

The Grandmothers

We have silenced our grandmothers
Mies Bouwhuys

We have silenced our grandmothers.
Rumpelstiltskin forgotten,
the spinning-wheel covered in dust.
Snow White's mirror is tarnished,
the words stuck in its throat.
Jack the Giant Killer's medals
are stuck at the back of a shelf
in a backstreet pawnshop.

The grandmothers are silent.
There is a house agent's sign
outside the Beast's castle;
the garden is choked with overgrown roses
that bloom no longer.
The doctors have decided
to switch off Sleeping Beauty's
life-support machine:
seven desolate dwarfs
wander the back lot of Universal Studios.

We have silenced our grandmothers.
The Princes, pale or otherwise,
have departed,
the Princesses having married
millionaire Texan playboys;
the last dragons are preserved
as endangered species
in distant game-parks;
the last grandmother unheard
above the neon blare
of TV screens.

Carol

Wreath the bay and twine the holly
Let the herald angels sing
In pubs replete with fake brass lamps
And contract carpeting

Bring the gifts of endless shopping
Supermarkets open late
Fill the freezer to abundance
Leave the hungry to their fate

Fairy-lights deny the darkness
Christmas trees on every lawn
Somewhere in a freezing stable
Another orphan child is born

Deck the halls with flameproof tinsel
Hang the cards on nylon thread

Praise the Lord the New Year's coming
Thank the Lord the old one's dead.

The New, Fast, Automatic Daffodils/Two

I wandered lonely as a lonely cloud
I wandered lonely as a lonely crowd
I wandered lonely through the lonely crowd
an all-at-once, a one-time-only crowd
a host, a cloud of roots that clutch
a host, a crowd of looks that touch
that floats on high o'er vales and hills
that floats on, high on booze and pills
as stoned and lonely as the daffodils.

It's the New Fast Automatic Daffodils /Two
It's a new fast automatic poem for you
it's a wander through a lonely crowd
it's a wander through a host, a cloud
of new fast plastic daffodils
of automatic, variomatic thrills
that flash upon the inward eye
a sudden flash of inner thigh
FULLY AUTOMATIC
that inward, inner-city thigh
FULLY AUTOMATIC
and then my heart with pleasure fills
and dances with the daffodils
FULLY AUTOMATIC
the variomatic, inward daffodils
FULLY AUTOMATIC
the new
          fast
                automatic
                      daffodils.

The Day of the Dead, Hope Street

silence in Hope Street
silence in stony places
after the agony in St. Luke's Gardens
silence

'Ladies and Gentlemen
Señors y Señoras
for one night only
The Simultaneous and Historical Faces of
Death!'

fade in F.X. laughter
faint boxy sound of cheap guitars
songs torn from dried-up larynxes

they dance
ignoring double yellow lines
around crimson traffic signs
ROAD CLOSED
noseless faces laugh elated
clattering pasodobles
echo from the walls of the Philharmonic Hall
GRAN VERBENA DE CALAVERAS
stretched across the street
before the Cathedral's crowned nosecone
pink   turquoise   ice blue
sequinned skirts whirl
faster and faster farandoles
a lone black cat
picks her way between the dancers
heaped marigolds scream orange defiance

the Consul white suit crumpled
lounges in the doorway of the Philharmonic Pub

tequila in hand
bloodred tropical sunset
reflected in his eyes

trauermusik:
above the rattle of firecrackers
raucous chords scrawled
by bony fingers
above high strings
the pure clear sound of a viola

a tall, black-bearded Irishman
a short-haired girl in black ski-pants
scarlet tin-soldier jacket
peer through the crowd
as white elbows snap
doff their sombreros
dance round their hats
skeleton señoras
elegant in pink-and-white boas
watch stately
their pinstriped husbands
tap silverheaded canes to the rhythm

confetti hurled in the air
hot breath
the smell of mescal   enchiladas
pink   white   yellow
cellophaned flowers forgotten underfoot
a black-and-white sheepdog
sniffs our flesh round rotting bones
lifts its leg against traffic cones
calaveras   calaveras   calaveras
prance   castanets   click
quicken the rhythm of the dance

at dusk
the carnival departs
hands yellow with the dust of mimosa
hair braided with crimson carnations
a trail of bright red petals
trodden beneath her limping feet
echoing distant laughter
along the empty street

Wish You Were Here

Throughout his adult life Adrian's home was, resolutely, Liverpool. He was not a native – he came, travelled here, fell in love with this scabby whore of a city/this golden girl of a City, 'dangling her landing stage in the water'. Many of Adrian's contemporaries moved away from Liverpool, found and fell in love with other places. And yet amongst those same contemporaries, Adrian – the one who remained – was the true cosmopolitan. Where many, myself included, merely went to places, sometimes stayed in places, came back from places, Adrian travelled, journeyed, sojourned; and however apparently mundane or exotic his destination, he would always find riches, gaudy baubles, exquisite treasures all of which he sent or brought back in postcards, poems, stories, pictures and bags of glee.

Was Adrian a poet first and painter second or vice versa? I heard him asked the question a number of times and on each occasion deftly sidestep it with the asser-tion that first, second and third he was the front man in a rock band. The question is, anyway, misguided and to raise it surely misses the point. As many of the poems in this and other sections vividly testify, Adrian Henri the poet and Adrian Henri the painter were one and the same, the painter's eye and the poet's tongue a bonded, inseparable harmony whether turned upon the dreich of a northern afternoon, the shimmering African plains or the dull unlovely street suddenly kissed and made fine by the step of a smiling girl.

Once, in Galway sharing reminiscences of Adrian, an Irish friend mused, 'Adrian Henri – he'd the poet's tongue all right. But he'd also the painter's eye.' There was a pause in which heads were nodded in concurrence before another friend added, 'And not only that, he'd the rock star's gift with the women.' Another pause and this time, a thoughtful shaking of heads. And then the awed, respectful whisper – 'The lucky bastard!'

So he was. And so were we who sometimes travelled with him.

Willy Russell
Liverpool, 2007

America

A Confidential Report to Dr Bertolt Brecht on the Present Condition of The United States of America

'America, fabulous meltingpot!
God's own country!
Just called by the initials,
USA,
Like everybody's boyhood friend, incapable of change!'

Bert Brecht, 'Vanished Glory
of New York the Giant City'

TWA Flight 707 1300 hrs from London arr. NY 4.30

late pounding down pier 22   12.IV.69
blue sky soft ribbed sandclouds

Loew's Midtown Motor Inn.   8th Ave between 48th and 49th Streets, New York,
*   NY 10019*

sunset helicopters Hudson river
from my 11th-story window

waking to red-and-black funnels behind the buildings
noise of rockdrills police sirens waking me every morning
RHEINGOLD, THE TEN-MINUTE HEADACHE

terrible heat like an oven between the buildings   14.IX.69

On Broadway
3 black prostitutes   13.IX.69
beautiful

standing like the Supremes
about to sing 'Stop
in the Name of Love'
as I walk round the corner
Al Kooper tired nervous cowboy
at home
playing the electric keyboard

The Dixie Restaurant: Closed for Jewish New Year

Television: hideous quizgames

day   Batman

and   The Addams family

night   stockmarket quotations

Castle: for Malcolm Morley

man in a sailboat
placed there by the invisible hand
motionless for ever
not wondering why
stones as real as painted clouds
at the hard white edges the dream fades
in the hard white empty studio

for John Clem Clarke

drifting along with the tumbling tumbleweed
in the St Adrian Co.
painted Cavaliers quietly watched me get pissed
bright lights Coney Island on Bleeker St
yellow taxi home

Pennsylvania Landscape from the Air

parallel brown treemossed hills
curving away straight like tiretracks
bluemisted to the horizon
cottonwool pinches of clouds
near the ground
brown slow river muddy with islands
turning highways
green/brown Stella stripes of fields
cars ponds mirrors hidden among the trees

5.X.69

WHEN IN HISTORIC VALLEY FORGE STAY AT THE
GEORGE WASHINGTON MOTOR LODGE

gleaming peacock butterflywings
inside plastic blocks
in a New York shopwindow

a fly falling down vertically
before my eyes
kicked twice
and dying
whilst cleaning my teeth
in a Holiday Inn in Kent, Ohio.

5.X.69
for Allen Ginsberg

Allen stumbling walk guide to the nightworld
buying egg creams at the allnight Gem Spa
dirty faded sign FIVE-SPOT
trashcans car engines mattresses
meeting a man carrying a shining bikewheel
in dark wiremesh Tomkins Square

strange beautiful cracked voice
autoharp dulcimer songs of Innocence and Experience
lambs dancing on the hillsides
poet burying his face in the rainsoaked grass
dark streets distant glass breaking
home in a yellow taxi

the girl who sits next to me in the hotel coffeeshop
furcoat worrying about her acne eating a hot fudge sundae

Ohio Landscape from the air

patterns of township
clumps of red gold orange trees
pale clay streaked
round green ponds reflecting the sun
rows of parked cars
shining like child's glass beads in the sunlight

6.X.69

I sit on a bench on the sidewalk
outside the sad laundromat
red-and-black birds darting in cages
in the petshop next door

The poet dies, killed by the child's snowball.

NYC 21.X.69
for Jean Cocteau

wanting to give you Taglioni's jewelbox.

images for
Joseph Cornell

brown velvet
nine crystal ice cubes
jewelled alladinscave
between the spaces
when you lift them out

constellations wheel
outside the windows of the Hotel de l'Univers

pharmacy:
butterflywings and histories of Cleopatra
stored on the gleaming shelves

wooden parrots yawn
in the deserted shootinggallery
floodlit skaters in Rockerfeller Plaza
light on iceblades
dyed unreal brightgreen trees

                                        images for Mike Evans

AMERICAN WIG CO. COVERS THE WORLD

WORLD HOUSEWRECKING CO.

The Venus Brassière Co.

'what a shame they don't have Jurgens lotion in Russia'
– think of all those Red hands they could have avoided

DANTE'S INFERNO
STEAK TONIGHT

Also
Sprach Zarathustra
dawn spacemusic
for frozen breakfasts

phone call to you $32 plus tax

beautiful sad distant littlegirl voice
black cat waiting beside you in the darkened hallway

                                                                                28.X.69

across the Mystic bridge to Salem
blue schoolgirl's witcheyes blue stockings
past giant cactuses
leaning towers of Pizza
plaster cattle grazing on floodlit lawns

                                                                        Boston 17.X.69

loving you
in identical Holiday Inn bedrooms
only the landscape outside the window
different
(changed once weekly)

                                                                                 1.XI.69

night landscape to NYC from the air

for the American painters of the
            1950s: MR/AR/BN

frozen tundras of cloud
caught with gold from the setting sun

dark hard horizonline
redgold edge
darktoned lakes
below the line
sprinkled with pale yellowgreen lights

bright neon jewelry
laid out on plump blackvelvet display cushions

small white things shattered at my feet twice, mysteriously
twice crossing Sheridan Square, unsure
turning to your beautiful black embrace   for Ted Joans
poetfriend from Timbuctu and Edinburgh   NYC 7.X.69

proud Norseman   for Moondog
standing on the corner of the Avenue of the Americas   Detroit 6.XI.69
spear horns unpraised
heavy trafficsounds
fog on the Hudson
roars of rockdrills
behind blind eyes waves of music crashing through his head

  'But
Now, to get jobs, the 22-year-old
Girls sniff cocaine before going out
to win a place at the typewriter'

                                              – Brecht, 'New York'

Mike and I looking at the Chrysler building
and suddenly
water falling on us from the sky
people staring at us
two men dripping wet
walking down neon electric 42nd Street
on a sunny afternoon

night subway home at 3.30 people sleeping on benches

laughing brownfaced girls from New Orleans
giving us grapes on the Staten Island Ferry

night   for Brent, Tanis and Sonny Rollins.
Manhattan bridgeline   Detroit X.XI.69

hearing in my head
lonely saxophone in the night
from the Williamsburg bridge

                                        images for James Nutt and his painting.

desolation in a Chicago hotel bedroom.

Amerika the blank staring face behind the pinball machine
eyes painted on the glass
Lake Michigan beautiful uncaring
tall towers into the night
green Frankenstein light in tunnels
painted mouth screaming soundlessly
behind the unwinking lights
orange falltrees shed their leaves sadly
along the expressways

'Ah, the women's voice from the phonographs!
So they sang (keep those records) in the Golden Age!
Euphony of the evening waters of Miami!
                                                    – Bert Brecht

Bellefontaine, Ohio
'Monument to the 1st concrete pavement in America 1891'

INTERSTATE 75 blue-and-red highway shield

                                        Michigan – Ohio 13.XI.69

leaves burning on suburban lawns
darkred Rothko barns white clapboard houses
familiar M1 pink homelight across evening fields

the secret storm in Columbus, Ohio

neonlights through the snowflakes
cosy porchlights through the trees
across snowcovered lawns

Sue standing at the top of the stairs
her shadow on the wall
waiting

old men trudging through leaves in the park
blind musician gone from the streetcorner for the winter
men fixing Christmastrees in front of skyscrapers

NYC 20.X.69

the poet falls
blood trickles from his head into the snow
darkred beautiful
as roses in evening gardens
between Mobile and Galveston.

Detroit 6.XI.69
for Guillaume Apollinaire

157

A Song for New Year's Day

Dawn drenched into sodden day
pheasant wings whirr into morning
high stones guard the hills
villages quietest under the winter sun
circled yews by rotting iron vaults
dripping to misted afternoon
late light dies on puddles along lanes
with no turnings:
now the season turns
mistletoe stamped underfoot on the bar-room floor
the hills encircle, the valleys enfold
mist tucked between like bedclothes
Christmas-lights down village streets
guard the darkness:
now is the solstice
the shortest of days
raise high the glass against the night
light fading over the hills;
still the tall stones await a winter sacrifice
black hills dark with heather
drink up forget the ghost in the chimney-corner
rattle the lock in the door
the watching and the waiting
dance in their turning
alehouse and graveyard, watcher and walker.

Drinker and dreamer move in their courses
turn with the seasons
drink with the dancers
wait for the new year's slow expiation.

Landscape, Ulster

(for Edna and Michael Longley)

What
do these fields
conceal?

the sheep graze as elsewhere
first signs of spring in copses
the hills the farmhouses
all normal enough

are there boobytraps
behind every blade of grass?
exploding snowdrops?
assassins lurk in every hedgerow?

only the crows walk fatter along the verges.

Two Seasons

early spring:
a brimstone butterfly
imitates
the primroses.

late summer:
bees busy in the balsam
peacocks pose
cabbage-whites drift among thistledown.

from Silvington Songs

(for Ken and Elspeth Gill)

2
A Song in April
(another song for A.E.H.)

The buds of April bursting
Into the flowers of May
Await a cold November
Forgotten in the clay

The lambs of April playing
Are due to die in June
The loves of April laughing
Will come to tears too soon

The loves of April blossom
And last a summer long
Come close, for chill October
Will come to end the song

Come close, my love, and tell me
April will never end
That daffodil like gorse-bush
Will last to the year's end

That lambs will dance for ever
And lovers never part;
Come close upon the pillow
And still my restless heart.

3

dawn light
shutters the ceiling

words throb
the millstream spills
into the still air
outside,
snowflakes
powder against huddled daffodils
faded confetti under churchyard yew trees
linked by birdsong

waking,
to memories of midnight sheep
eyes apprehensive in the fitful lamplight
silent Easter madonnas
glittering nativities
golden offerings of heaped straw
lambs,
loosely inhabiting their woolly suits
suck at friendly fingers
outside,
a cock crows twice
denying this birth-day

the mare,
stretched patient on the stable floor
the foal wet and shivering beside her
in the hard electric glare
outside,
yellow bramble-leaves from purple tendrils
against white rhythms of dead branches

now,
as the blue light
brightens on the ceiling
cries of crows dancing their courtship
lamb and foal leap unknowing in the fields

bridegrooms wait at every church-door
mayblossom immanent in the hedgerows

in this bloodstained straw is all our beginning
struggling to rise again uncertain to the light
remember
that harsh midnight
on this beginning day.

An Incident at Longueville

(for John and Ann Willett)

1

It is early afternoon. Late summer sunlight fills the street.
The sound of bells. She waits outside the Café Tellier.
She has been there since the bells in the slate-spired church
last rang. Dark hat, almost like a beret, pulled well
over her eyes. The shadow of the awning of the Café Tellier
falls at an acute angle. She waits with hands in pockets
head down does not see the shadow nor hear the laughter
of the five girls walking arm-in-arm beneath the little railway bridge
at the end of the street.

2

Bells again. It is le Quinze Août and the town closed
for holiday. Still she waits head down unseeing.
The laughing girls have long since gone. Baked mud and brick walls
reflect the heat. The gravel of the forecourt in front of the Café Tellier
stirs beneath her foot. The shadow of the awning has moved,
imperceptibly. The crossing-bell and the heavy breath of an approaching
train. The foot turned out towards us taps unconsciously on the gravel
to its rhythm.

3

Catching her breath slightly from the uphill walk,
too hot in the thick coat with the fur collar, her
tight shoes resent the cobblestones. She walks into
the Place du Calvaire, then waits in the middle of the little street
behind the monument. A child watches, incurious,
from outside his garden gate, blue school smock on despite the feast-day.
In the background a tall fir tree overgrown with ivy. The ochre
walls of wood-framed barns. The shadow of the Cross

falls on the brick wall behind it, the arms a shallow angle
to the single band of yellow brick. Its two metal supports are shadowed
like a corollary.

4

She stands as before, head down, no longer hearing
or counting the bells. No traffic turns the steep corner
by the Cross. Hands still in pockets, she stares at the base
of the sunbrick wall. She does not see nor think of the frozen bronze agony
whose harsh shadow shifts yet again as we watch. Lengthening
shadows in a red-tiled kitchen await her return.
Le Quinze Août, Feast of the Assumption, the festive tables
are ready. Soon she will walk out of the Place du Calvaire.
In the dark forest along the valley a white château dreams.

5
She walks away from us down the Rue de Belgique. The shadow
outside the Café Tellier has lengthened almost to vertical.
Round the corner by the épicerie trots a white horse,
bridled but not saddled, led by a fat, unsmiling workman,
cigarette and bleus de travail. The man who rides the horse's back
is made of flowers.

from **Poems from Germany**

'… Songs of a wayfarer …'

1

Giant hogweed takes over suburban gardens,
unobtrusively,
murmuring of *lebensraum*
VORSICHT BISSIGER HUND
thunders from every gateway,
only the foxglove wanders free;
the evening light
is decorated with oakleaf clusters.

2

Primroses lurk in the darkness of cupboards
the bird has been deflowered, feathers drift
across stained bedclothes. A sad girl
prepares the grave of the last amaryllis
märzebecher   *maiglöckchen*
the sound of the last train
drowned by the sound of the fountain.

3

GEOFF BOYCOTT we love you
Christopher Isherwood is a fucking liar
written on The Wall
rabbits run free
in the grey Vopo wilderness
body soft in the lamplight
shy voice on the telephone
a small crimson bear
left at Bahnhof Zoo
in the early morning.

4

Perfumdeo/a found poem

Spring dream
Yellow moon
Wild flower
Green summer
Blue river

(Deodorant names from a supermarket shelf)

5

Dream

The blue dream rises gently from the ground,
its pink mouth agape
hovers above the crowd
bumps gently against an ochre dream
drifts towards the sun
which is ringed with rainbows

Max Beckmann, 'Der Traum' (1927)

7

I bring you from Germany
tangerine-flavoured lipsalve
called KISS ME
a chocolate hare for Easter
and a pack called, simply,
Anti-Baby Condoms.

9

Sunlight on the Alster. A boat called Charly
bobs behind your head. Words left
unsaid. Shade of umbrellas, willows;
a dazzle of green park, thick brush-strokes

on the water. Empty glasses on the orange table.
You teach me to say *zahlen bitte.* Flotillas
of baby ducks. Swans turn, languid as
middle-aged sunbathers, stirring to do the other side.
The minutes to go like the lapping of small waves
as the ferryboat arrives.

Colden Valley, Early Spring

Frost persists to afternoon
on one side of this valley
icicles depend
the shadow of the other bank
moves inexorably to the diagonal
never allowing the daylight to fall
here.

Rich textures of lichen
green elephant-hide of beeches
palest sienna of bracken
beckon in the March sunlight.

Here there are only stones of purest marble
frozen in small streams.
The brightest afternoon
cannot dispel the darkness
beneath these stunted branches.

Souvenirs d'Anglesey

Valse

1

the sea,
and first sight of storage-tanks
early blackberries
and a white goat
grazing on a guest-house lawn.

2

pale moon
in an immovable blue sky

bright Pompeian light
on symmetries of abandoned kilns
votive shapes
of bleached brickwork.
slow
suck
of the tide
perspectives of curlews
and the distant sound of seagulls.

3

double-shaded
rockpools
crimson, viridian
dreams
against slow rhythms
of monotone weed.

4

white sheep
clipped
neat as topiary
three dark-green sandpies
against the sunlit grass.

5

a sprig of weeping willow
from where his brave leg lies buried
in some corner of a foreign field.
Before painted perspectives of a harbour
haunted by sea monsters
the Fifth Marquis (as
Pierrot) waltzes nervously
with one elegant, leather limb.

Morning Landscape, Tattenhall

Two saturated wreaths of poppies
at the foot of the War Memorial.
Behind the drenched coppice, tiny
waterfall, tangled winter branches,
a haunted grange still dreams.
Over the bridge, and two sudden beams
of sunlight from the broken sky
touch the distant hills,
like an Annunciation.

Garden, Giverny

Delphiniums, sweet williams,
purple gladioli,
against yellow asters, marigolds,
the whirl of sunflowers;
glimpsed pink walls against emerald shutters.

A bamboo-grove
lurks in the shadows by the lily-pond,
patient as a tiger.
Lovers kiss on a Japanese bridge
watched by the bearded phantom
from behind the willows,
sad as a blind girl in a summer garden.

Morning, Belfast

for the girls of St. Louisa's, Belfast

Brown-uniformed
blue-ribboned
Children of Mary
Siobhan and Maureen,
Mary and Siobhan
your faces should adorn
the gable-ends of walls
ten feet high along the Falls.

Morning, Sunset Heights

Dogs bark
down the canyon.
A crow croaks
its complimentary
wake-u-up
croak-o-gram;
a hummingbird sips
from the hibiscus.
Bougainvillea
glows. The sun
hides behind thin mist
'Have a nice day'
ready on his lips.

Four Studies of Dieppe

For the painter Nicholas Horsfield

1

light arrives in the harbour
like a monarch at a painter's door
the brush poised to trap
like a lobsterpot.

2

apple-orchards moult pink into summer
an excitement of melon against green lawns
the haze of sardines grilling
hydrangeas pushing in at the night window.

3

paint glitters like mackerel spilt on the quayside
the breath of ferries and fishingboats
caught against an impasto of cliffs
framed in an oval sunset.

4

burnt sienna scumbled against zinc white
where only the green-capped stones, gaunt as Frankenstein,
remember the suck of boots,
the crunch of landingcraft.

Souvenirs

(for John and Anne Willett)

Chocolate sardines, torn election-posters MAR
CHAIS, huddled sheep before a distant sepia
view of Pourville. The yellow-and-grey world
of Lords and Ladies on the wallpaper in
the *lingerie.* Lemon light. Night hydrangeas.
The smell of the ferry, scrubbed mussels
deep blue in a white bowl in the electric kitchen,
where moths beat against the windowpane. Blinding
rain that wipes away the cliffs at Etretat.

Green depths of evening *sous-bois*, tall trees
that shutter the light along the banks outside
the villages. A black workman's suit, a sailor's cap
bought beside St Jacques. *Oeufs de Pâques.*
Andouillettes, and mackerel cooked with driftwood
on the beach. Each stone I have brought home
since 1968. Late light across the harvestfields
from Ambrumesnil. Cattle dream, creamy as caramel.
The smell across the valley from the Nescafé factory.

The tall gingko tree that split ten years ago,
one twin trunk that still lies overgrown,
immutable as memory.

Fallen Appletree, Normandy

It lies on the grass,
winded,
orange and yellow fruit
hung like Christmas lights
in the bare, brown,
summer branches.

We take a photograph.

The image develops,
slowly,
in winter darkness.

Garden, Barlaston

Rich leather leaves of whitebeam
scattered white side up,
evergreen sheen of rhododendron,
turned hopefully to the November sun:
the willowherb's white cursive
writes summer's testament
against sleek holly,
dying privet.

Death Valley

Yea, though I drive
airconditioned
through the Valley of the Shadow
of Death,
still I fear
its ancient evil;
the unblinking rocks,
the unforgiving heat:
Nissan and Mitsubishi
do not comfort me.

A Poem Instead of a Postcard

Dear Janine,
                    A postcard from the edge
of Africa. *Impressions d'Afrique.*
Only a week, and already memories
come and go, regular as the ferry,
regular as thoughts of her, despite
the catwalk grace of girls on the beach,
each with an invisible load on her head;
skin so black that it refracts the light,
as evening sprawls across the harbour,
staining dark red walls a darker red.
I sit on the terrace for hours. The fish
is delicious. Can't wait to paint
the flowers. I want to stay.
                                        love,
                                            A.

The Parsonage, Haworth

In the earth, the earth thou shalt be laid,
A grey stone standing over thee;
Black mould beneath thee spread,
And black mould to cover thee.

                                        Emily Brontë

Gravestones piled deep as fallen leaves,
trodden into the sodden ground;
last consumptive flush of Autumn
in the sycamores;
a kissing-gate swings disused
in the bitter wind.

Cries of crows, rattle of rain,
on the nursery windowpane;
insistent tick of the grandfather clock,
insistent tock of the stonemason's hammer,
stammered epitaphs
swathed in lichened green.

It is not the stone that eats their bodies,
but the black spring that runs through them
that feeds the dark sarcophagus.

A glimpse of sun
sudden as a blush suffusing soft cheeks;
pale blue eyes
calling through blonde coppices of hair
across the dimpled moors.

From an Antique Land

1

Cows browse
in the Basilica
black-and-white
against black columns.

Eyes blue
in the basalt darkness
glow like poppies.
Umm Quais.

2

She waits patient at the gate
for us, tattooed patterns
on her face, weathered
as the desert.
          The child
who clings to her black skirts
wears a Mickey Mouse T-shirt.
Quasr Hamam al Sarak.

3

Schoolgirls in long blue dresses,
whitescarved heads,
blossom in the lunchtime street
like bougainvillea.
Amman.

4

A chameleon
ignores the laws

of Justinian
on a granite wall.

Quasr el Hallorat.

5

Mirages shimmer
false mirages of polythene
shimmer too.

Umm el Rasas – Kerak.

6 *Bedouin*

He picks his way
along the track
carefully
not separating
the sheep
from the goats.

7 *Petra*

Pink palaces
beyond the dreams of postmen,
rose-red rocks
beyond the dreams of palettes,
wait to be reborn
beyond the dark passage.

8

I smear my mouth with Vaseline
my lips dry
for lack of your kisses.

(for Catherine)

9

The Caliph sits in majesty
above the dancing-girls, the graffiti;
the painted Zodiac awaits
Eid, and the rising of the moon,
a sugared almond in the sky.

Quasr Amara / Petra.

10 *Aphrodite*

She dances
– tiny, golden,
voluptuous –
to unheard music
in a museum case
in Liverpool.

Jordan / Liverpool
April–October 1991

Dark Gate

We wait
at the dark gate
of the sea

amethyst   lapis lazuli

slow sound of emerald olive-green ultramarine

silver-grey syllables
hiss along the shingle;
bladderwrack and seagrass,
starfish and periwinkle,
cast upon the tide
where pale foam rides,
violet swell
beyond the harbour-bell.

the cry of sea birds unheard
beneath the glaucous deep.
slow wash of words
turquoise   cobalt   indigo
sifts through ochre sounds,
whispers of razorshells, sea anemone,
tells of the evening star,
far above, bright
as mother-of-pearl,
as the girl left at the quay.

wrecks sway silent,
slumber in the umber depths
of the sea.

Dreamwreck

In our separate worlds
we call each other lover,
though oceans, seas, borders,
inches, miles or only words
apart

Cast upon broken spars,
clinging desperate
amid torrents of sound;
each sentence
a 'lifeline
or deathrope'
before we drown.

In our separate words
we call each other lover,
though inches, miles, borders,
oceans, seas or sometimes worlds
apart.

Sea Dawn

'sea birds are asleep'
cuckoos rest in alien nests
sleep is on the land.

Faintest fret of sound
shadows silver harmonies
of just-beginning day.

Becalmed,
grave counterpoint of wave on wave
dawn ripple of strings
gentle obbligatos
of laver, carrageen,
dulse and kelp
drift unseen
where the bowsprit swings.

Ballad of the Thames and Medway Barges

Aidie Ailsa Agnes Mary
Abergavenny Alice Ash
Asphodel Atlantic Atlas
Beyond the bay where breakers splash

Barbara Jean and British Lion
British Oak and British King
Bluebell Bessie Hart and Blackfriars
Lost to sight where mermaids sing

Centaur Challenger and Clara
City of London Coronation
Creeksea Clare and Castenet
Stream towards their destination

Dorcas Doris and Dundonald
Dabchick Daisy Little Devon
Edith Eva Esther Emma
Mirrored between sea and heaven

Foxhound Fortis Flower of Kent
Gertrude May and Golden Eagle
Giralda Globe and Good Intent
Shadowed by the lonely seagull

Iverna Irex and Jim Wigley
Inflexible Juliet John Bayley
Kathleen Kindly Light and Klondyke
Breast the waves as sails fill gaily

Lady Daphne Lady Mary
Lizzie Laura Lily Lloyds
Marguerite Marian Matilda
Skirt the bank the shoal avoids

Nelson Northdown Nellie Austin
Onward Oak and Olive May
Pall Mall Plover and Plinlimmon
Sail into the breaking day

Scotia Sepoy Santanita
Sirdar Swallow Swift and Squeak
Thelma Tortoise Tyne and Thistle
Urged on by the mizzen's creak

Valkyrie Victis and Verona
Violet Sybil Volunteer
Wheatsheaf Waterloo and Warwick
See first sight of land appear

Barges of the Thames and Medway
Agnes and Zabrina fair
Safe at last to ride at anchor
Folded in the harbour's care

Ketches Shrimpers Tramps and Bawleys
Folded in the harbour's care.

Nocturne, Venice

4 a.m.:
in the darkness of Harry's Bar
the ghost of Ernest Hemingway
sits sipping shadows.

A propos de Nice

1

After Matisse
picnics beneath olive trees
the Sunday light cuts shadows
like painted paper

2

A mackerel sky
above the fishing boats
Dufy waves
feather the bay

3

Nouveau riche
against the night
yellow lights
gleam on the bosom of the Corniche

4

Beignets, Socca, Bagna Cauda
tastes bright as bougainvillea,
the night smell of datura.

Black Mountain Poem

Before
the Brecon Beacons
bracken beckons,
the road to the black hills
calls the tune,
a bus ruffles the hem
of Queen Anne's lace.

In the still air
bright parachutes
hang on the wind's every word,
sheep songs heard
from far below.

Wordgathering,
images caught in clumps
on barbwire fences,
not neatly laid
like drystone walls;
elusive as the organ-calls
of birds,
rich as the pony's mane
you said looked like
Tina Turner's hair.

Below the square,
the clock-tower,
the river runs,
guiltless and deep
as things not yet written:
beyond the poem
the Black Mountains wait.

La Recoleta, Buenos Aires

red stockings
bloom in the afternoon
red carnations
laid on a grey tomb

white lace
white flowers
pink artificial roses
Della Robbia madonnas
a neat brass handrail
down the steps to the underworld

Luis Angel Firpo
in dressing gown and boxing boots
PLAY WOMEN
behind his bronze head

broken windows
stained sepulchres
withered flowers
old CocaCola bottles
walls crumbled
a coffin's green handles
open to the air
chaste angels
avert their gaze
from prurient towerblocks
carved daffodils
around a child's sepia portrait
blue   red   yellow plastic buckets
carved baby lips
suck hungrily
at a stone breast

FAMILIA DUARTE
still cry for her
a bronze virgin
in a bronze rosegarden

shadows of dark cypresses
float on a white mausoleum
grey as dusk
cats haunt the passageways
hooded figures mourn
the closing of the gates
the passing of the light.

Out of Africa

1

'Where is here?' Light fights
through dead serrated leaves
twisted ochre trunks
slides off gleaming green
lands triumphant on the wet grass.
The poets talk of exile.
In the Botanical Gardens
the Ficus Religiosa offers a prayer with every leaf.

2

cheerful eloquence of street markets
pears balanced elegant on top of other pears
casual as acrobats
chiming discords of coriander and chile
MOTHER IN LAW EXTERMINATOR
MOTHER IN LAW HELLFIRE
'Ebony Frogs on Special'
striking workers from The Blue Waters
chant and dance
before the greygreen sea.

3

Brandeplankry Verbode
you leap and splash in the multiracial surf
where ships queue at the horizon.

4

The spiderweb of E. T. SECURITY
guards against enjambement,
stolen syllables. Uniformed men

with guns guard the entrance
to every stanza. Yellow
enamelled signs protect
end-stopped lines.

5

Bloodorange sun
above pale lacquered sea.
Tiny hands at 2 a.m.
outstretched for pennies.
Peace and Reconciliation.
'They've just found some more graves
in KwaZulu/Natal...'
Thunder rumbles overhead.
The sky is overcast. The moon
is the wrong way round.
I cannot see the Southern Cross.

6

You are green dawn over red mountains
the gentle sex of zebra and nyala
quick grace of the impala
kopjes of the Drakensberg
the taste of sunset over sandstone gates
the Milky Way that fills my eyes
from sky to sky, stars tangled
in all your branches.

Landscape, Umfolozi

(For the National Association of Painters in Acrylic)

6 a.m. Mist brushed wet-on-wet
into pale cobalt sky, monestial distance.
A touch more medium. Foreground
oxide of chromium, splattered sap green,
in between a zebra's stripes, carefully redrawn,
off-white against brown-black. At the back
a chatter of baboons burnt umber into the branches;
a lone hyena skulks into sage-green.
In the foreground, quick dabs, the shy eyes
of impala. Catch them quick
before they dry. Through the thorn trees
black bulk of a rhino threatens the stretchers,
the composition. Brushes washed
at the waterhole. The image fades
in the eight o'clock haze.

IF YOU WEREN'T YOU ...

24 Collages No. 6, Mulligatawny Soup Painting (Homage to Andy Warhol), 1964

24 Collages No. 4, Clayton Squares Painting, 1964

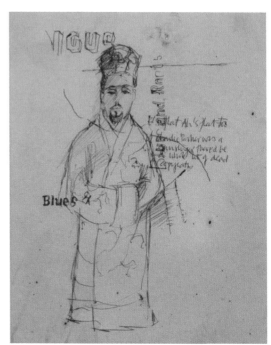

Mingus, 1961

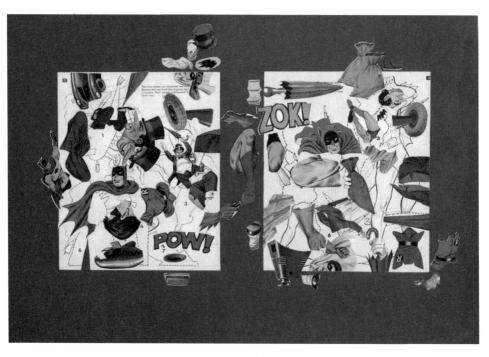

Batcomposition, 1967

Kop II, 1977

Dream Palace (Homage to Ferdinand Cheval), 1988

... *Who Would You Like To Be?*

His heart point north
but his soul point south
he paint with his tail
and he poem with his mouth –
that Adrian cat

Adrian was a great hero-worshipper. Art was his life and he celebrated artists of all kinds, while being modest about his own lovely work. He was also a great friend and comrade, my favourite Blues Brother on many wild poetry gigs.

On a stormy night, when the poetry organizer had advertised us for the wrong night, or absconded with the cash, and all around were melting in dismay and anger, there would be a deep, spreading chuckle from the corner, as Adrian greeted disaster like an old friend – with a huge warm hug.

Adrian Mitchell
London, 2007

Me

if you weren't you, who would you like to be?

Paul McCartney Gustav Mahler
Alfred Jarry John Coltrane
Charlie Mingus Claude Debussy
Wordsworth Monet Bach and Blake

Charlie Parker Pierre Bonnard
Leonardo Bessie Smith
Fidel Castro Jackson Pollock
Gaudì Milton Munch and Berg

Belà Bartók Henri Rousseau
Rauschenberg and Jasper Johns
Lukas Cranach Shostakovich
Kropotkin Ringo George and John

William Burroughs Francis Bacon
Dylan Thomas Luther King
H. P. Lovecraft T. S. Eliot
D. H. Lawrence Roland Kirk

Salvatore Giuliano
Andy Warhol Paul Cézanne
Kafka Camus Ensor Rothko
Jacques Prévert and Manfred Mann

Marx Dostoievsky
Bakunin Ray Bradbury
Miles Davis Trotsky
Stravinsky and Poe

Danilo Dolci Napoleon Solo
St John of the Cross and
The Marquis de Sade

Charles Rennie Mackintosh
Rimbaud Claes Oldenburg
Adrian Mitchell and Marcel Duchamp

James Joyce and Hemingway
Hitchcock and Buñuel
Donald McKinlay Thelonius Monk

Alfred, Lord Tennyson
Matthias Grünewald
Philip Jones Griffiths and Roger McGough

Guillaume Apollinaire
Cannonball Adderley
René Magritte
Hieronymus Bosch

Stéphane Mallarmé and Alfred de Vigny
Ernst Mayakovsky and Nicolas de Staël
Hindemith Mick Jagger Dürer and Schwitters
Garcia Lorca
                    and
                              last of all
                                        me.

Batpoem

(for Bob Kane and The Almost Blues)

Take me back to Gotham City
      Batman
Take me where the girls are pretty
      Batman
All those damsels in distress
Half-undressed or even less
The BatPill makes 'em all say Yes
      Batman

Help us out in Vietnam
      Batman
Help us drop that BatNapalm
      Batman
Help us bomb those jungle towns
Spreading pain and death around
Coke 'n' Candy wins them round
      Batman

Help us smash the Vietcong
      Batman
Help us show them that they're wrong
      Batman
Help us spread democracy
Get them high on LSD
Make them just like you and me
      Batman

Show me what I have to do
      Batman
'Cause I want to be like you
      Batman
Flash your Batsign over Lime Street
Batmobiles down every crimestreet
Happy Batday that's when I'll meet
      Batman

Adrian Henri's Last Will and Testament

'No one owns life, but anyone who can pick up a frying pan owns death.'

William Burroughs

To whom it may concern:

As my imminent death is hourly expected these days/
car brakes screaming on East Lancs tarmac/trapped
in the blazing cinema/mutely screaming I TOLD YOU SO
from melting eyeballs as the whitehot fireball
dissolves the Cathedral/being the first human being to die
of a hangover/dying of over-emotion after seeing 20
schoolgirls waiting at a zebracrossing.

I appoint Messrs Bakunin and Kropotkin my executors and make the following
provisions:

1   I leave my priceless collections of Victorian Oil Lamps, photographs of
     Hayley Mills, brass fenders and Charlie Mingus records to all Liverpool
     poets under 23 who are also blues singers and failed sociology students.
2   I leave the entire East Lancs Road with all its landscapes to the British
     people.
3   I hereby appoint Wm. Burroughs my literary executor, instructing him to
     cut up my collected works and distribute them through the public lavato-
     ries of the world.
4   Proceeds from the sale of relics: locks of hair, pieces of floorboards I have
     stood on, fragments of bone flesh teeth bits of old underwear etc. to be
     given to my widow.
5   I leave my paintings to the Nation with the stipulation that they must
     be exhibited in Public Houses, Chip Shops, Coffee Bars and Cellar Clubs
     throughout the country.
6   Proceeds from the sale of my other effects to be divided equally amongst the
     20 most beautiful schoolgirls in England (these to be chosen after due delib-
     eration and exhaustive tests by an informal committee of my friends).

Witnessed this day by: Adrian Henri Jan. '64
James Ensor
Charlie 'Bird' Parker

Five Translations from Alain Bosquet

1

Hear the volcanoes
talking of thirst
Come back soon to the mangotree
as you would turn back to God.
The lake absolves you
for having been made flesh.
In the place of the soul
choose a hummingbird.
Hear the volcanoes
devour their skeleton.

2

You wheel above
the hovering vultures
above the vulnerable palmtrees.
You will punish the sky
if the earth trembles at morning,
if the ocean heaves up at midday,
spewing out its heart among naked cliffs.
You hover
not daring to live
in the reality of three hundred swamplands.

3

A crack at the heart of Reason.
A glance uncertain as washing in the rain.
A poem too weak
to hold its words.
The shadow of a gallows between shadows.
On the beach an ear
listening to all the universe will not say.

Each night, you marry the unknown
each morning, the unknowable.

4

Be Berenice, don't worry
It's an honour for Jean Racine.
Claude Monet, a paintbrush away,
Begs you to pose among the waterlilies.
Pergolesi and Lully fight for your face,
Their only harmony.
If you leave, a slap in the face for Europe,
Dream of Rimbaud as you would dream of thirst.
Draw near to this carriage:
Guillaume Apollinaire has sworn to wait for you
until the day the Rhine stops flowing.

5

Bougainvilleas climb
like scars.
Why is the star too civilized?
Beaches drunker than acrobats.
At the end of the jetty, the fortress
shakes her thousand cormorants.
The cruel sand sits on memories
to stifle them.
How many towns
have hanged themselves in the forest?
You, the carnivorous gate.

What Were You Thinking About?

Dressed and then dressed again
what were you thinking about
undressed

I left my mink in the hallway
and we went into the desert
We lived on love and cold water
we loved each other in our poverty
we even ate our dirty linen in public
and on the black sand tablecloth
the sunlight spread its golden dishes
We loved each other in our poverty
we lived on love and cold water
my body your freehold property.

Translated from Jacques Prévert

Père Ubu in Liverpool

A Fragment

Time and Place:
Liverpool now

Dramatis Personae:
Père Ubu
Mère Ubu
Palotins
Liverpool bird
Mods
Man in bowler hat

SCENE ONE
(Père Ubu is discovered walking round the corner of Lewis's.)

Ubu (mopping brow):
By my green candle, we are excessively fatigued. (Sees bird standing underneath statue.) Young lady, having recently disembarked from that which crosses the water of the Mersey, we are taking our Royal Person to your splendid Cathedral, which will serve as our Phynancial Quarters, being of suitable magnificence.

Bird (aside):
State of 'im!

Ubu:
… could you therefore direct the here-present Master of Phynances to the building we have named?

Bird:
Yerwhar?

Ubu:
Hornsgidouille, I cannot communicate with her. I shall try once more…
Mademoiselle?

Bird:
Ooer!

Ubu:
Shittr! WHERE ARE WE?

Bird (comprehending):
Oh! Lewis's.

Ubu:
Ah. And that is no doubt a statue of Mr Lewis?

Bird (pointing upward and giggling):
What – *dar*? No. Dat's 'Scouse'.

Ubu:
And who is that?

Bird:
It's a statue of a feller with no clothes on and, er, all the fellers meet their birds under it and when it's wet the rain drips off 'is thingie and it looks as if he's… (dissolves into giggles)

Ubu:
I see. And where are you going, my dunderheaded maid?

Bird:
I'm meetin' me friend Mary and we're goin' to The Cavern.

Ubu:
Ah, yes, I had heard there was a Cavern in the town.

Bird:
I'll 'ave ter go now – tarar!

(She hurries away, watched by Père Ubu. When almost offstage she drops her handbag, shouts 'ooer', picks it up again and exits.)

SCENE TWO
(The scene changes to Hardman Street. Père Ubu is discovered toiling up the hill, followed at a distance by Mère Ubu and a number of Palotins.)

Mère Ubu:
Oh, Père Ubu, you big bag of shit, why don't you ask someone the way?

Ubu:
Silence, Mère Ubu, or I'll wring your horrible scrawny neck. (Sees a crowd of Mods leaning against the wall outside The Sink Club. Speaks to the nearest one.) Tell me, sire, could you direct me to that edifice known as the Cathedral?

Mod:
Yerwhar?

Ubu:
Hornsgidouille, shittr, can no one here speak a civilized tongue?

Mod:
Now then, la, yer wanner watch dat languidge yer know.

Ubu (to Mère Ubu and party):
Ignorant savages!

Mod:
Yer lookin' for a spot of lumber, la?

Ubu:
Lumber?

Mod:
You know – a bit of a barney, a punch-up, a KO job like.

Ubu:
Do you dare to challenge the mighty Master of Phynances himself to battle? The great Père Ubu, King of Poland, Count of Sandomir, Emperor of Liverpool! By my green candle, shittr, sire, a hideous fate shall be yours. Torsion of the nose and ears, extraction of the eyes. Insertion of the Little Piece of Wood into the Nine Entrances of the Body…

Mod:
All right den. I've got me mates here. (Pushes Ubu.)

Ubu:
Forward, Palotins, let the shittr-hook do noble battle! (The Palotins rush forward

waving lavatory brushes and start fighting with the Mods. One Mod falls to the ground. Others have got a Palotin on the ground and are putting the boot in. Père Ubu retires to the rear and shouts encouragement. One of the Mods sees him and rushes towards him.)

Mod 2:
I'll get the big feller.

Ubu:
No no don't hurt me I'm on your side Liverpool for the Cup I Love You Yeah Yeah Yeah Long Live King Billy. (By this time he is cowering behind Mère Ubu's skirts. Mod 2 pushes her aside and seizes him.)

Mod 2:
Yer dirty Prodestant bastard! (Butts him.)

Ubu (on ground):
Ooh, I'm dying. Our Phynancial nose, pride of our magnificent body, is irreparably broken. Help me, Mère Ubu!

Mère Ubu:
Help yourself, you bloody great baby.
(The Mods run off. Palotins help Père Ubu to his feet.)

SCENE THREE
(Outside the Philharmonic Hall. Père Ubu, Mère Ubu and the surviving Palotins trudge along Hope Street. Enter a man in a bowler hat, morning suit, briefcase, rolled umbrella etc.)

Ubu:
Ah! At last a worthy-looking citizen. Obviously a Rentier, a man of substance in this city. Perhaps I shall now get some civilized directions… Excuse me, sire, but I and my entourage have walked for many hours and our Royal feet are exceedingly sore. Could you perhaps direct us to that which has heretofore been known as the Cathedral?

Man:
Yerwhar? (Ubu collapses.)

CURTAIN

Salad Poem

(for Henri Rousseau le Douanier)

The sun is shining outside
Henri Rousseau (Gentil Rousseau)
The sky is blue
   like your skies
I want to paint the salad
on the table
bright crisp green red purple
lettuce and radishes, ham and tomatoes
Paint them like your jungles
Gentle Rousseau
I want to paint
   All things bright and beautiful
   All salads great and small
I want to make
   Blue skies bluer
   Green grass greener
   Pink flowers brighter
Like you
   Henri Rousseau.

Poem for Roger McGough

A nun in a Supermarket
Standing in the queue
Wondering what it's like
To buy groceries for two.

Wild West Poems

1   Noon:
        2 tall gunmen walking slowly towards each other down Mathew St.

2   *And then*
        He tied her up
        And then
        He lit the fuse to the dynamite
        And then
        And then
        AND THEN ALONG CAME JONES …'
                                      (for Leiber/Stoller and the Coasters)

3   William H. Bonney alias Billy the Kid hitches his horse to a parkingmeter
        strides through the swing doors into Yates Wine Lodge. Barmaids slowly
        back away from the counter. Drunks rush out into Charlotte Street. He
        drinks a glass of Aussie White and strides out, silent as he came.

4   *Poem for Black Bart to Leave Behind on a Stagecoach*

        I hope you ladies ain't afraid
        Of the wicked man who made this raid
        But I'm like nature quick and cruel
        Believe me, gals, I need them jewels.

5   The Daltons riding down Church Street/Bullets ricochet off streetsigns/
        windows full of cardboard Walkers bottles shatter/Bob Grat Emmett
        thunder across trafficlights at red/hoofbeats die away clattering down
        Lord Street.

Hello Adrian

(for Adrian Mitchell)

Hello Adrian,

    This is me, Adrian. I hope you had a nice Christmas as it finds us here. We had that nice Mr and Mrs Johnson to tea who's president of something but they didn't like those yellow people from across the road. Christmas had us a bit worried but Santaclaus in his big Red Cloak came down her chimney and now all those cards with cribs on won't be in bad taste after all. Very strange things have been happening lately. People keep falling off cliffs and into bed with me. Last night I met Paul McCartney in a suburban garden wearing a moustache drawn by Marcel Duchamp. I keep wanting to sign shelves of tins in Supermarkets. Everytime I go for coal the coalplace is full of dead Vietcong. Birds have eaten the berries off our plastic holly. I think it's going to be a hard winter.

    Today is New Year's Day, should Auld Acquaintance be Forgot? I don't know but my stomach feels funny. I have sent messages to the leaders of the various parts of my body asking them to end the fighting NOW. There's no shillings left in the meter we'll have to roast a leg of pork over the gasfire. Someone's left the front door open O My God we might have had thieves murderers nutters queers anyone coming up here. Now someone's taken the cat and left a shovel instead.

    People keep offering me nebulous schemes for making my fortune in various of The Arts. A girl told me 'I had a dreadful time on Christmas Day, Uncle Gerald kept putting his hand up my skirt.' There were huge punch-ups in Woolworths on Christmas Eve. I have seen the entire Works of Charles Dickens on the telly this Christmas … Oliver Twist going to see Miss Havisham with Tiny Tim … Scrooge skating with Mr Pickwick … Pip stealing handkerchiefs to give to Little Nell … I can't stand it any longer if those Chuzzlewits call again we're *definitely* not at home. I'm making New Year Resolutions again but I'm not likely to meet her *this* year either. I'm going to have my poems on Cash's Woven Nametapes put inside schoolgirls' gymslips. I'm going to treat white Rhodesians as equals. I've forgotten all the others already.

    I think Spring must be coming. She brought me a bunch of plastic violets yesterday. I can hear the noise of the ice floes breaking up on the bathroom floor. There's still no one waiting by the waterfall: I looked again today.

    I really must close now as the Last Post is sounding, so hoping this finds you as it leaves me love to all at No. 18 from all at No. 64.

Adrian

Poem in Memoriam T. S. Eliot

I'd been out the night before & hadn't seen the papers or the telly
& the next day in a café someone told me you were dead
And it was as if a favourite distant uncle had died
old hands in the bigstrange room / new shiny presents at Christmas
and I didn't know what to feel.

For years I measured out my life with your coffeespoons

Your poems on the table in dusty bedsitters
Playing an L.P. of you reading on wet interrupted January afternoons

Meanwhile, back at the Wasteland:
Maureen O'Hara in a lowcut dress staggers across Rhyl sand-hills
Lovers in Liverpool pubs eating passionfruit
Reading Alfred de Vigny in the lavatory
Opening an old grand piano and finding it smelling of curry
THE STAR OF INDIA FOUND IN A BUS STATON
Making love in a darkened room hearing an old woman having a fit on the
        landing
The first snowflakes of winter falling on her Christmas poem for me in
        Piccadilly Gardens
The first signs of spring in plastic daffodils
on city counters

Lovers kissing
Rain falling
Dogs running
Night falling

And you 'familiar compound spirit' moving silently down Canning St in a night
        of rain and fog.

Pictures from an Exhibition

(Painting and Sculpture of a Decade '54-'64, Tate Gallery, London, April–June 1964)

No. 54 Jean Dubuffet, 'Déclinaison de la Barbe' I, 1959

'as-tu cueilli les fleurs de la barbe?'
Jean Dubuffet I wander the dark pebbles of your mind picking beardflowers.

No. 73 Joseph Cornell, 'Hôtel de l'Etoile'

cool pillars of the hotel / in the
night outside the stars are always
so white / the sky is always so
blue / silver moon waiting patiently.

No. 84 Mark Rothko, 'Reds – No. 22', 1957

SCARLET
ORANGE
ORANGE
ORANGE
SCARLET
CRIMSON
SCARLET

No. 291 Robert Rauschenberg, 'Windward', 1963

printed oranges are painted
painted oranges are painted

Angry skyline over the gasworks
A Hawk sits brooding inside a painted rainbow.

Nos. 10–13   Josef Albers, Studies for 'Homage to the Square', 1961–2

look.

see.

long ago.

now.

No. 314   Bernard Requichot, 'Sans Titre – Chasse de papiers choisis'

chasse aux papillons:
'Here Be Tygers' –
– the fruit in the tin has a thousand eyes.

No. 349   Jim Dine, 'Black Bathroom No. 2', 1962

black splashes on the white walls
interrupting the commercials
TURN ON THE GLEAMING WHITE SINK
AND POEMS COME OUT OF THE TAPS!

No. 139   Victor Vasarely, 'Supernovae', 1959–61

BLACK IS WHITE
BLACK IS WHITE
WHITE IS BLACK
WHITE IS BLACK

No. 50 Louise Nevelson, 'Sky Cathedral III', 1960

Black
  Black
Black
  Boxes
Black
  Light
Black
  Moonlight
Black
  Emptiness
Black
  Dust
Black
  Boxes
Black
  Black
Black

No. 247   Richard Diebenkorn, 'Ingleside', 1963

Look through the Supermarket window / up the highway
the hill rises steeply / hoardings and magnolias bright
in the sunlight / white walls black freeways trafficsigns
at intersections / green lawns dark hedges / colours
clear and bright as the packets in your wire basket.

Out of the Railway Wardrobe

(for Rob Conybeare)

Out of the wardrobe. Out of the darkness. Out of the railway distance. Behind the suits carefully preserved in mothballs for the next wedding funeral divorce or christening the seats of the trousers gleaming grey-striped or navy-blue in the faint light from the end of the tunnel. The tunnel whose sootysmelling breath still holds the memory of long-dead steamtrains. Chugging over points, the blackened sandstone walls stretching up to the light. Regular rows of strip-lights against the walls and clumps of willowherb growing in crevices far above. Behind the slightly faded wine-coloured evening dress, the wine-coloured satin dance shoes with diamante heels, the black afternoon frock with the pattern of tea roses, the overhead gantries meet the rails at the precise point of infinity. Out of the warm musty darkness the childhood slightly scented smell of fur-coats against your nose tickling you as you breathe in eyes accustomed to the rustling dark the line of light round the not-quite-closed door as the sound of metal wheels accelerating across level-crossings grows nearer and nearer.

Out into broad daylight your unexpected city faces. Red marsupial stranger poems clutched warm in the little pouch.

Out of the wardrobe out of the junction boxes out of the serge and mothballs the silk and fur out of the sound of whistles and platform-trolleys. Out of the wardrobe … wardrobe of dreams wardrobe of desires … wardrobe of upholstery smelling of tobacco-smoke … wardrobe of the emptiness of stations wardrobe of memories … wardrobe of discarded female underwear … wardrobe of darkness … wardrobe where farewells hang in the glass and cast-iron roof … wardrobe of broken-down patent-leather tango-time dance-pumps … wardrobe with hidden illicit dusty books on top wardrobe of perspectives wardrobe of forgotten encounters … wardrobe of crashed carriages splintered sleepers the crumpled metal rusting in summer rain … wardrobe of cheap hotel-rooms of stains on unwelcoming sheets … wardrobe of immobility wardrobe of rushing autumn landscapes past windows … wardrobe of old-fashioned tennis-racquets and withered rubber bathing-hats … wardrobe where one gossamer floats in the railway carriage sunlight wardrobe where one pigeon limps along the platform … wardrobe where dreams lie wrapped in tissue-paper like faded orange-blossom … wardrobe where dreams wait endlessly outside Crewe Station … wardrobe where dreams hang crumpled their buttons missing … out into daylight where dreams float away on the wind tinged with petrol fumes … out into bright afternoon red marsupial stranger lost in a wilderness of concrete flyovers.

From the Loveless Motel

(i.m. Elvis Presley)

a lovepoem for America

night
remembered
saxophonelights
of the Williamsburg bridge
Caffè Roma
cannelloni   cappuccini
bowers
of artificial flowers
across the morning sidewalk

WALK
DON'T WALK

San Gennaro
patient in a dusty shopwindow
gazes down on the little street
waits for his day of triumph

WALK   DON'T WALK

giant puffs of smoke from a huge cigarette
against the sky
                masks
Hallowe'en masks everywhere

GENUINE IMPORTED JUNK $4

lone
black
saxophone-player
outside the church of St Thomas
bright blaze of red-and-white

reared against blue
A train, A A train

WALK

Our Lady
smiles
her 3-D Polaroid
smile

WALK
DON'T WALK
YIELD

curling deltas into brown savannas

EXIT THROUGH THE DOORS WITH THE FLASHING SYMBOLS

electric sound of cicadas
key-limes   mangoes

FOLLOW THE RED SYMBOLS

tiny rainbow lizards
mourning-doves too slow for cats
sandpipers skitter busy across white sand

FOLLOW THE BLUE SYMBOLS

pelicans come up gulping
Alice in a pink-and-white gingerbread wonderland
dimpled brown bringing Budweiser

WALK
DON'T WALK
FOLLOW
FOLLOW

lovebugs die in each other's arms on windshields

THE WORLD'S MOST UNUSUAL DRUGSTORE

                      mermaid show 3rd floor
masks
orange masks

THE FLASHING SYMBOLS

Our Lady of 51st St
her halo of stars
eclipsed by the neon dazzle
of Times Square

WALK

lost in a wilderness of rusting railroad tracks
tumbleweed drifting
seeing America from underneath
the peeling underside of flyovers

one more hangover
and a thousand miles to go

YIELD

THE LOVELESS MOTEL

redeye   corngrits
shadowy bellhops
weep
silent tears

Dusty Roads
2 a.m.
painted shadows on the wall
"swingin' doors"

a barstool
and a jukebox"
the girl I love
2000 miles away

WALK
DON'T WALK

Dusty Roads, take me home

dark
in his niche
in the ochre desert
S. Francisco
rests
amongst handmade, lace-edged,
satin pillows

FOLLOW THE
smiling hostess like Connie Boswell

FLASHING SYMBOLS

beautiful
barefoot naiads in McDonald's
jumping up then settling like seagulls
wet hair
thin T-shirts over just-formed breasts
('they'd lock you away
for 100 years')

DON'T
WALK

prickly pears
jojoba   manzanita
rusted automobiles
nestling in canyons

snow among aspen-trees
Inspiration Rock
jukebox playing
them sweet country sounds
again

YIELD

turquoise
and one pink
crosses
a tumbleweed
blown against a turquoise-tinselled grave
curled photographs
faded plastic flowers
crêpe-paper stars and stripes
bleaching in the sunlight

FOLLOW

'the white dove
of the desert'

Our Lady
pale blue knitted shawl
over her painted dress
her feet heaped
with offerings
        babies' shoes
        hospital ID tags
        colour photos of servicemen
        little embroidered pillows
        votive images of Robert Kennedy
        tiny silver arms and legs
        one
        child's yellow sock
        names on scraps of yellowed paper

her
gilded halo
caught by candlelight

DON'T
WALK

masks
orange white Hallowe'en bright
saguaros   savannas
red deserts
mapleleaves through mist

FIGHT FIERCELY

invisible 3-D rays
pour from her wounded palms
lost
above the neon signs
above the desert sunlight
from the concrete grotto
from the dusty storefront

YIELD

By Grand Central Station
I have sat on commutertrains
and thought of you

WALK

THE FLASHING SYMBOLS

'the loneliest arms
in the world'
on an empty jukebox

my Lady of
The Loveless Motel
be with me and remain with me
now and for always
black-clad
desk-clerk
at the gleaming counter.

September Poem

(i.m. Mao Tsetung)

The East wind blew bitter in the night
quiet in the morning
dead chrysanthemums in suburban gardens.

Will the flowers
planted at the graveside
bloom another year?

And will the East wind
blow so fierce again?

Poem i.m. P. G. Wodehouse

Darkness at the Drones Club
dust settles silently on mahogany chairbacks
a ghostly footman shimmers in
black-edged card on a silver salver.

Penny Arcade

(for Joseph Cornell, NYC)

Utopia Parkway:
Blind arcades. Bouquets
of shipwrecked flowers.
Melted majesty of the sunset. *Salsa verde.*
The city from 100 storeys
open to the night. WE HAVE RUSH
shout the walls, the highways.

Utopia Parkway:
Night tide. Beauty convulsive as
eyes lit by sea-light. Outside
the white hotel the stars
are printed in their course.
666 in neon
above the frozen, haloed city.

Utopia Parkway:
Parrots wait
patient as pharmacists. Drifts of dawn
like ice-floes against tall towers.
Miss Jasmine glitterqueen
declares the daylight,
hearts scattered on the broken kerbstones.

A palace of dreams waits untenanted
A parkway of light up the morning street.

New York City Blues

(for John Lennon)

You do not cross the road
To step into immortality
An empty street is only the beginning

The words will still flow through you
Even on this cold pavement,
Are heard in some far place
Remote from flowers or flash-bulbs.

In that city, on Gothic railings
Dark against the snowy park
Still a dead flower, a faded letter,
Already one month old.

'Life is what happens to you
When you're busy making other plans,'
This empty street
Is only the beginning.

Here, in your other city,
Riot vans prowl the December dark,
Remember angry embers of summer,
Familiar ghost guitars echo from stucco terraces.

Meanwhile, in the Valley of Indecision,
We rehearse stale words, store up expected songs,
Celebrate sad anniversaries.
Flowers and flash-bulbs. Cold pavements.

You do not cross the road
To step into immortality
At the dark end of the street
Waits the inevitable stranger.

The Long and Wider Road

Elegiac fragments for Roland Penrose

'If you are lying your finger will be trapped
If you tell the truth it will lead you
out to the other side

                      to an island'
                      Roland Penrose 'The Road is Wider than Long'

1
Autumn destroys:
a shadow
pushes itself across the garden
the mingled smell of chestnuts and excrement
cars trapped in tunnels
patient as rats on a dissecting-table
glimpsed dimples
in the midst of traffic-jams
the road
longer than wide
hurtling landscape into white landscape.

2
A pipe without a name
that proclaims
THIS IS NOT MYSELF
shelf of forgotten expectations
discovered cupboard
of discarded dreams.

3
Miserable miracle
that sits just out of sight,
crawls in spidertrails
against the light,
lurks
at the edge of comprehension.

4
Erotic phantom just down the street
shrouded in bright blue honeysuckle
veil briefly lifted,
tantalized by the lamplight;
DESIRE written in the stars
reflected sudden in her eyes.

5
THIS IS NOT A POEM
screams the poem
soundlessly.

The Birthday Party

for Willy Russell

Happy Birthday, Dennis. Forty years, eh?
Talkin 'bout my generation. Here's a present.
The latest John Denver: hope you haven't got it
already. What's that? Someone sent you
a fake bus pass? Probably those kids again. Typical.
Jane was saying only the other day
how well you looked. Thought you were never going
to ask. Not *red*? Hear that, Jane? Big Bold Burgundy…
Black mark. Sainsbury's. Gewurztraminer.
Here's looking at you, kid. Many of 'em.

You didn't think I'd forget, did you, Frank?
Spanish red. The man in Quicksave said it was all right.
What do you mean, you've stopped counting? Go on,
open it. Cheers. What? Oh, that. Yes,
I've done it: Compare and Contrast Shaw's *Pygmalion*
with *Educating Rita*. What do you mean, I can't say

I preferred *My Fair Lady*? You know, from the side
you look a bit like Michael Caine, Frank. If only
you'd smarten yourself up. Life begins at forty. Cheers.
Happy Birthday. Anyway, what's wrong with *My Fair Lady*?

I don't know. Lend us your lippy. Do you like it streaked
like this? Some feller's birthday. Sharon Louise from the office
told me. A writer or something. Funny thing to be.
Wonder what he does for a living? Quite dishy, really. For a writer.
Proper clothes and that. Giz a drink. Me seams straight? Cheers.
Wonder what the talent's like? Someone's fortieth, they reckon.
Forty. Bloodyell. It's like being an O.A.P. Hey,
what if all the tarts are his age? Grab-a-granny time.
Like a night down the Sausage Factory. Lend us your comb.
I'll wipe it after. What's this? Don Cortez. Cheers.

What's that, Mrs. Johnstone? They would have been forty today?
Mustn't dwell on the past. Have another Guinness. Cheers.
Cheer up, it's a party. I don't know. Some writer feller.
Plays, someone said. Nice woman at the next table. Really brown.
Says she lives in Greece. Wonder who she's talking to?
State of that one there. Supposed to be a teacher. Asleep under
the table. Nice girl with him, too. Ssh. They're making an announcement…
Here's a Valentine from Shirley, and one from Rita, too,
a kiss from the Daughters of Albion, and a Birthday poem for you.

The Bell

The bell
tolled all afternoon
we did not send to ask
for whom.
It told of flowers
heaped in a goalmouth,
red and blue scarves
heaped together at an altar;
it told of
eyes like T.V. screens
haunted by last night's images,
tears dried by the April wind.
As the flags at half-mast
stirred overhead
the deep bell
still tolled in our heads
long after the light had gone.

A Portrait of the Artist

(in memoriam Sam Walsh)

In a forgotten attic smelling faintly of soot
propped against a peeling wall,
there is a painting,
wrapped in a moth-eaten tartan rug.
Next to it, linked by cobwebs, flakes of plaster,
the mummified bodies of spiders,
there is a battered, dark red portfolio
with black, triangular corners,
the black tapes that used to fasten it missing.
In it the artist kept his dreams.

There is a dream
of painting a giant replica of the Pier Head
to be installed at Woodside Ferry;
of one-man shows held weekly
on the pavement at Cazeneau Street market;
of a portrait of Ingrid Bergman
her haloed, backlit hair
painted as tenderly as Alfred Hitchcock,
the shadow across her cheekbone
painted as delicately as Michael Curtiz;
of himself playing the John Wayne part
in a remake of *The Quiet Man:*
there is a final dream
the artist did not dream,
of paintings of Saddam Hussain
and General Norman Schwarzkopf,
huge as war memorials.

Beneath the rug
there is a painting.
It is a portrait of the artist,

unfinished.
The artist, black beard trimmed neatly,
high cheekbones, dark hair falling
across his forehead,
looks out of the picture
which he has forgotten.
Behind him the model lies,
waiting patiently,
her shell-pink body
painted in the manner of Lucas Cranach.
A wisp of spray-paint
seems to indicate a room
not unlike this attic.

The artist gazes out at us;
carefully painted highlights catch
the glimpse of mockery in his eyes.
He does not see the gleaming, skeleton hand,
painted in the manner of Hans Holbein,
place an opened bottle of whisky
silently on a table by the easel.

The dust in the attic stirs for a moment,
then settles; a few tiny motes
catch the late afternoon sunlight.

Camille Claudel

Someone has stolen her God.

Her smoothest flanks untouched.

She sleeps like a doll
on the dunes above the shoreline:
the cruel birds,
under guise of nesting,
gather, gather.

Clair de Lune

(for Laurie Lee)

The poet
points his white stick
at the moon.
'Is it full?'
he asks.

Honeysuckle, Butterfly, Rose

And her far seas moan as a single shell,
And her grove glow with love-lit fires of Troy
D. G. Rossetti, 'Venus Verticordia'

Golden aureole, palest areola
more delicate than roses,
hair haloed with brimstone butterflies

Honeysuckle, butterfly, rose,
apple and dart

Heart cleansed of all
but the sight of white breasts,
prouder than envious flowers

Apple and dart,
honeysuckle, butterfly, rose

Coarse stamens strain
for that dark grove where far seas moan,
as in a single shell

Honeysuckle, butterfly, rose,
apple and dart

Pierced by her eyes wherein no glimpse
of love-lit fires, sudden as marigolds
found in a winter castle

Apple and dart,
honeysuckle, butterfly, rose

Virgin and Magdalen,
apple and dart,
Eve, Lady Lilith;
only to taste the forbidden secrets

Honeysuckle, butterfly,
butterfly, rose.

The White Ball

(after Ivan Puni: 'Construction With White Ball', 1915)

'What is this?'
the eager museum lady asks;
'A Ball!' 'A Ball!'
chorus the children.
She tosses them words –
'synthesis', 'construction',
'colour' –
they wait in vain
to catch a white ball.

André Breton at Varengeville

In the round tower where doves dream
her name is the beginning of hope. Unable
to forget the moment in the Rue Lafayette,
chance encounters haunted
as the man who constantly meets himself
in the cinema. Her eyes the colour of fernleaves,
filled with echoes of regret
that hang in the cast-iron roofs
of railway stations, eyes that speak
of city streets
VINS   BOIS   CHARBONS
of the magic of dark passageways,
tantalising as cream silken promises,
the statue in the suburban park at dusk.

'L'Etreinte de la Pieuvre';
In the darkened picture-palace of your dreams

it seems that only the fearless poet
(and his intrepid helper Sandy McNab)
can rescue the lovely Ruth
from the octopus tentacles, the satanic gaze
of the fiendish Doctor Wang Poo.

Sloping evening light from the West
fills the hollow between her breasts
where the steep path leads to the sea;
last lingering trace
of that delicate smell,
the taste of rockpool, seashell,
the pink embrace of sea-anemones,
carried on the wind.

Her name is the beginning of hope,
but only the beginning.

Now,
I watch her lying in the sun,
like a cat watching a butterfly.

La Mer

Claude Debussy at Pourville

Footsteps in the snow
across the white page
the sudden swell
of bells beneath the sea
cathédrale engloutie
white notes glide
like sails
across the darkened harbour.

Siren-song of your eyes
green stream
that drags me down unseen
Ondine
seaweed parts   reveals your smile
brown arms embrace
drowned   last memory
of your face
feux d'artifice
fade against night waters.

Blues for Slim

(in memoriam Slim Galliard)

Cement mixer don't putty-putty no more
Cement mixer don't putty-putty no more
Cos my man Slim has gone to Lethe's shore

There's silence down on 52nd Street
Silence all down 52nd Street
Couldn't hear the King of Vouti's beat

Went to Laguna, watched the tide come in
Went to Laguna, watched the tide come in
Searched the beach but couldn't see my Slim

Now I'm dunkin' bagels back in Liverpool town
Dunkin' bagels back in Liverpool town
Thinking of Slim as the Mersey sun goes down

Cement mixer don't go putty-putty no more
Cement mixer don't go putty-putty no more
Cos my man Slim has gone to Lethe's shore

A Brief Reflection on Poetry

(for Miroslav Holub)

The poem
reflects briefly on itself.
The blackboard
behind it
in the Music Room
briefly reflects it:
breve, semibreve,

quaver, semiquaver;
in the silence after the poem
the ghost of a violin
quavers briefly.

Memphis Sunset

You forgot to remember to forget
how the sun came up at 78 r.p.m.
a battered panel truck
parked in the studio back lot
until the blue moon set over Kentucky.

All around the world
every boy and girl heard the news
there was good rockin' in Memphis
put on their rockin' shoes.

But this time they made you a mountain,
a mountain you really couldn't climb.
Impossible. Its rhinestone slopes,
Lone Star peaks, impassable.
Impassive avalanches of applause,
snowblind in the spotlights.

An echoing voice
says you have now left the stadium,
scuffed blue suede shoes
forgotten in the dressing room.

Outside,
the black stretch limo waits.

A Landscape for Adrian

For Adrian Mitchell, anno aet. 65

> *'…a walk across a field*
> *of buttercups and landmines'*

To walk ten years on
find the piteous earth torn by landmines
reclaimed by buttercups
poppyseeds await patient decades
to spurt bloodred across forgotten battlefields
grass picks its quiet way
through the tarmac of out-of-town hypermarkets.
It is maybe Maytime
with drifts of bluebells   the smell of wild garlic
and a golden retriever bounds forever
from the woods at the edge of the poem
towards her master…

Eco-Poem

For Roger McGough

'I'm saving energy'
he said,
not switching off the light.

Blue Morning

For the painter Lisa Cole Kronenburg

'Alluberall und ewig blauen
licht die Fernen!
Ewig… ewig…'
Das Lied von der Erde

Blue morning
passes the word from tree to sky,
child's eye open to the wide horizon;
a red river
courses the shining wetlands;
beneath, the sluggish, buried stream
bears memories of night rain, stormfall,
lost dreams.
Afternoon gleams gold
a solitary bluejay calls
below the waterfall,
a white bridal-veil
sighs into greenest depths.
Last light, Western sky
cerulean to ultramarine
eclipsed by charcoal trees;
night rain, stormfall, crowcall
drawn harsh against the coming dark.

Come Thaw

come thaw:
squirrels scatter from trees
scrabble in leaf-mould
where the snow's frail maidenhead
dissolves in dark water.
footprints – yesterday's blue death frosted birds –
obliterated patterns of absence
in the mind. jackdaws caw
more and more exultant from peak to rooftree
hurl their scarecrow shadowsplatters
into the wind.
spring come too soon:

subordinate clauses of drenched light
run their soft mouths
over the unexpected blue bottomless sky.
serried banks of sombre treetrunks
khaki branches seek their mirror-image in the lake
that clings to its crust of ice
black water tarnished as cold silver
or the fumes of antique auguries of yesterday's dead
whirled in a cold coagulated vortex.

when the day's pubic blush
sculpts all depths nearer
there is still a whirling background conversation
sticks and stripes
lips of bleak silence over the mouth of night.

Translated from Breyten Breytenbach

We Won't Forget That

we won't forget that
that we laughed, laughed that
much I'll never forget that
that we laughed that much, will we?
and we'll never forget be-
cause we laughed that much and
won't forget my God how much we laughed
and not and never forget that we laughed so
much because we were together
and laughed so much
we'll never forget that

From the Dutch of, and in memory of, Bert Schierbeek

Look, Stranger

What fascinates me about art is the process of metamorphosis. This is why I think the new twentieth century tradition of collage / assemblage so exciting. One thing I think is interesting about working today is a sort of awareness about how much personal content can go into a work of art and not violate its universal validity.

Adrian Henri, 'Notes on Painting and Poetry'

Peter Pan Man

When I was three I went to the end of the road to watch the King go by
there was a lot of people and someone in a plumed hat.
When I was six, I wore a striped woolly pullover and lived at the seaside
somewhere, far-off, people died in the streets.
When I was eight I volunteered to join the army
tin hat, corkgun and all,
and received a nice letter from the Colonel
('…wait until you're old enough,
and apply through the usual channels')
When I was thirteen I drew triumphant cartoons
showing weary Japs emerging from the ruins of Hiroshima.
When I was eighteen my horizon was bounded by Cézanne and T. S. Eliot.
After that I missed almost everything
(though vaguely aware of Bill Haley and the War in Korea)
Until suddenly, and too late, I put away childish things
painted HANDS OFF SUEZ on walls and cried as the tanks rolled into Hungary
marched on marches and sat down on demos
saw people under horsehoofs
was thrown into horseboxes by reluctant policemen.
Stalin, the Uncle Joe we sang about in the war
crashed from his pillar and lay at one with the dust
The Yanks, who gave me chewing gum and nylons to peroxide girls
no longer F.D.R. but J.F.K., red against the green of Deeley Plaza
and photos of black men torn by police-dogs
I drew votive images of Guevara
and mourned for the childhood dead in Spain
Trotsky, Bakunin and Mao told me
I didn't grow up I grew down
worried about the things I never saw as a child
(though I was told off once for laughing at
mufflered clothcapped men searching for a lost sixpence
and can remember hearing rows about money
I wasn't supposed to hear).

Yes, I'm the Peter Pan Man, the Boy Who Never Grew Up
Girls didn't like me
until
Wendy laid me gratefully under an oak tree when I was 21
Since I was 35 a hundred Tinkerbells have opened their pale magic
    thighs for me
But
Captain Hook, no longer Stanley Baldwin or Winnie with his big cigar
Waits in the wings, his teeth bared in a TV Colgate smile
plans to take away the medicines, drink the children's milk,
imprison my brother workers.
At the gates of Halewood and St Helens
The Lost Boys argue furiously
not hearing the steady ticking of the Crocodile
black homburg and toothbrush moustache
munching black men with tears in his eyes.
And a hundred bowler-hatted briefcase Pirates
tear down the streets of the Liverpool I love
clutching their plans exultantly,
The Wendy-House is blotted out by the dust of falling Georgian buildings
While I sing love-poems through microphones at Festivals.
The faithful Nana has been given the humane killer
her meat makes other dogs bounce with health.
Yes Mr & Mrs Darling sold us all down the line
in 1921 and '23 and '37
in '44 and '45 and all those times since
It's me and Tinkerbell and a few of the Boys
on our own now
Crouched behind rainbow barricades of broken promises.

Autobiography

IN MEMORIAM

Albert Johnson d. May 13th, 1970
Frances Johnson, née Potter d. May 16th, 1970
Emma Henri, née Johnson d. June 3rd, 1970
Arthur Maurice Henri d. June 29th, 1970

I

knocking on the nextdoor door. knocking. no answer. knocking. on their door. knocking. no answer. silence. then the sound of something moving slowly painfully inside bumping into things. door slowly opens. dirty matted hair darkshadowed crusted eyes wild growth of white hair and beard.

'who are you, then?'
the old twinkle in his redrimmed eyes
'come in, stranger.'
he moves slowly ahead hobbling on brokenslippered feet between objects too shrouded with dirt to be identified
'it's Adrian, love'
'who?'
'Adrian, your grandson, come to see you.'
room dark everything covered in soot sunlight barely able to get through the window, a small fire burning in the grate despite the heat of the day. she sits there like some terrible white vegetable unmoving there in her armchair: blind, unable to move, barely able to hear. sometimes she speaks, then dozes off again. her hands move occasionally twitch at the blanket round her waist. the Elsan bucket next to her dominates all the other smells in the overheated room. the only things in her life now: being lifted on to it, being lifted off it. sleeping. sometimes speaking to make sure you're still alive that the other one's still there. a nurse has come to dress his feet. she peels off the bandages. huge swollen sores on his poor twisted feet, feet that have been good for a lifetime of walking, working on a farm as a boy, working for the Corporation in the park across the road, pushing her in a wheelchair already semi-invalid for ten miles when they're on holiday. he

seems to doze away, as well, between sentences.

yes, they're all right. just a bit tired today.

no, I can't do anything. the girl from round the corner looks in of a morning to see if we need any messages.

money? no, we're all right.

we've got plenty of food.

space cleared on the oilcloth at the front of the table; all kinds of tins and packets and old cakes pushed back, disappearing in the dirt and cobwebs and shadows at the back. finally, helpless, I get up to go.

'all right, son, it's been nice seeing you. it does her good you know.

come and see us again.

don't leave it so long, next time. he's going now, love.'

'what?'

'he's going now.'

'oh, goodbye, love. Tata.'

bend over to kiss her. then struggle down the filthy littered unfamiliar corridor I know from childhood. out into daylight. grass growing between the cracked pavingstones. two days later they were taken to hospital. a week later he died. three days after that she died. I go to look at him in the funeral parlour. face white, strangely peaceful but they've shaved his moustache off along with the overgrown hair. why? it isn't him. why can't they leave him alone? his flesh is waxy, unreal, slight reddish purple contusions here and there like on a newly plucked turkey at Christmas. white satin fringed with purple tucked round him. floral tributes with little cards in Cellophane packed heaped round his coffin.

PART ONE 1932–51

1

flags and bright funnels of ships
walking with my mother over the Seven Bridges
and being carried home too tired
frightened of the siren on the ferryboat
or running down the platform on the Underground

being taken over the river to see the big shops at Christmas
the road up the hill from the noisy dockyard
and the nasty smell from the tannery you didn't like going past
steep road that made your legs tired
up the hill from the Co-op the sweetshop the blue-and-white-tiled pub
Grandad's allotment on the lefthand side
behind the railings curved at the top
cobblestone path up the middle to the park
orderly rows of bean canes   a fire burning   sweetpeas tied up on strings
up to Our House
echoing flagyard entry between the two rows of houses
brick buttresses like lumps of cheese against the backyard walls
your feet clang and echo on the flags as you run the last few yards
pulling your woolly gloves off
shouting to show Grandad what you've just been bought
him at the door tall like the firtree in the park
darkblue suit gleaming black boots shiny silver watch chain
striped shirt no collar on but always a collarstud
heavy grey curled moustache that tickles when he picks you up to kiss you
sometimes shouting angry frightening you
till you see the laughter in his countryman's blue eyes

2

round redbrick doorway
yellow soapstone step cleaned twice a week
rich darkred linopattern in the polished lobby
front room with lace runners and a piano that you only go in on Sundays
or when someone comes to tea
Uncle Bill asleep in his chair coming in smelling of beer and horses
limping with the funny leg he got in the war
Grandma always in a flowered apron
the big green-and-red parrot frightening you with his sudden screeches
the two little round enamelled houses on either side of the fireplace
big turquoise flowered vase in the middle
the grate shining blackleaded cooking smell from the oven next to it

big black sooty kettle singing on the hob
fireirons in the hearth
foghorns and hooters
looking out of the kitchen window
seeing the boats on the bright river
and the cranes from the dockyards

3

coming back the taxidriver doesn't know where the street is
the allotments at the foot of the hill
gone now
great gaunt terraces of flats
scarred with graffiti
instead
the redbrick houses tiny falling apart
the whitewashed backyard
where you could smell lilyofthevalley through the privethedge round the tiny
        garden
on your way to the lavatory at the end
empty dirty overgrown now
backdoor banging in the wind
grandmother grandfather both dead in hospital
one windowpane broken dirty lace curtain flapping
the funny little flights of steps
the secret passages in the park
pink sandstone steps overhung with trees up the side of the hill
overgrown or demolished
the big seacaptain's house where I used to go for a present every Christmas
forgotten
remembering
lying in bed
in the dark crying listening to my mother and father argue
wind banging a shutter
indoors somewhere

dead eyes looking out from flyblown photographs
empty mirrors reflecting the silence

4

RHYL SANDS:
your vision swept clear and bright by the wind that's wiping away the
      stormclouds
beach low and empty   pale blue sky   seagulls and one dog near the horizon
pebbles underfoot as clear as the wallpaper in seaside cafés
somewhere out at sea, a rainbow
the sad peeling offseason colours of arcades and kiosks
David Cox's 'Rhyl Sands' a tiny gem burning quietly in dirty Manchester
ghostly echoes of last season's chip-papers in the drifting sand

5

the house I lived in destroyed
now a glaring plateglass motorshowroom
only morning glories left on the fence by The Cut
narrow brickwall gorge
a thin trickle of smelly water now
not the raging torrent I once fell into coming home crying covered in pondweed
long low home violet slate roof two front doors with circular coloured windows
two garden paths big rockery border the rocks painted with orange spots
(I never found out why)
long rambling garden at the back with the woodyard behind
tall metal fence always coming down
whitewashed outside toilet for my lonely fantasies
echoing flagstone floor to the diningroom my mother said was haunted
rambling rosecovered fences lilactrees gooseberry bushes
appletree with a black cat climbing in it
Trigger the Wonderdog died aged thirteen in our new Council House
the old stone houses next door gone
the caravan full of noisy children

the ponies in the field across the road
the sound of donkeys distant in the brickyard field
the rusty whitewashed corrugated fence goals or wickets
by our backdoor where I used to play
gone
now
only a bald concrete patch
outside the brightlit nightglass windows

6

carrying my gasmask to school every day
buying saving stamps
remembering my National Registration Number
(ZMGM/136/3 see I can *still* remember it)
avoiding Careless Talk Digging for Victory
looking for German spies everywhere
Oh yes, I did my bit for my country that long dark winter,
me and Winston and one or two others,
wearing my tin hat whenever possible
singing 'Hang out the Washing on the Siegfried Line'
aircraft-recognition charts pinned to my bedroom wall
the smell of paint on toy soldiers
doing paintings of Spitfires and Hurricanes, Lancasters and Halifaxes
always with a Heinkel or a Messerchmitt plunging helplessly into the sea in the
        background
pink light in the sky from Liverpool burning 50 miles away
the thunder of daylight flying fortresses high overhead shaking the elderberry-
        tree
bright barrageballoons flying over the docks
morning curve of the bay seen from the park on the hill
after coming out of the air raid shelter
listening for the 'All Clear' siren
listening to Vera Lynn Dorothy Lamour Allen Jones and The Andrew Sisters
clutching my father's hand tripping over the unfamiliar kerb

I walk over every day
in the blackout

7

walking to the spring wood now a muddy buildersyard
footpaths then mysterious trackless intrepid
now suburban bungalowstreets gravel and tarmac
where the churnedup mud horsedung and puddles were
the woods alive with primrose and milkwort
wood-anemone and bright hawthorn
now a haven for gnomes and plastic waterfalls

8

darkgreen mysterious spaces under hedges
nettles along footpaths
to the Old Mill
stinging your legs
rubbing yourself with dock leaves
dog-rose and sweet briar
angelica and fennel
saxifrage starring the hedgerows

9

seeing into the clear water of the stream
the little wooden bridge
the fields rising on either side dusted with buttercups
darkgreen waterweed swaying
bright ripples echoed in gold below
pale brown blue grey pebbles on the pale sandy bed
eels and sticklebacks wriggling black away from your hand

10

lying on my back
listening to creeping insectsounds smelling the grass round me
looking at the sky
perspectives of sound
crickets   birdsong in the woods across the valley
clover ratstails celandines rabbitdroppings
feeling the movement of the earth
through my closed eyelids

11

water foaming and fizzing round your warm body
sudden rush upwards green light everywhere
sharp salty taste in your mouth your nose stinging
down again gasping your breath in
sounds rushing in cries of bathers distant children
the promenade the Pavilion bright like a postcard

12

sunlight on long grass
old lace curtains draped over raspberry canes
plump gooseberries cobwebbed in the shadows
the smell of lilac and woodfires burning
remembering the day I walked five miles to draw the waterfall
then found my pen was empty and bought a postcard with my last sixpence
and had to walk home
the postcard still pinned on my studio wall
frozen water falling white blood from a giant's side
walking after cocoa and buns and hearing of a poet's death on the radio
alone in the vast sad hospital
cowparsley patterning the hedges
light spilt like paint through the leaves

13

deep rosepetals on a close-cropt lawn
the scent of clover lying close to the earth
envious of the coolness under the green rosebush
a sad young poet thinking of her eyes the colour of shadows under the
    sycamores
shadows and a myriad insects creep in the tangled grasses
in the evening sunlight
filled with the sound of a thousand departing motorcoaches

14

remembering
the sudden pangs at corners
glimpsing the laughter of happy couples in the street
flat moonbranch shadows on the pavement
under a summer moon
or winter lamplight
nightwalks through the purgatory of half-built housingestates
the last-minute shifting of a cushion
for the seduction-scene that never takes place
for the waiting at the end of the privetlane
for the person who never comes

15

sad
boy-to-be-poet
head full of words
understood by no one
walking the dog
through the midnight bungalowworld
built over the
countryside
of his dreams

Poem for Hugh MacDiarmid

Dear Chris,
If I could only tell, like you
the kind of poetry I want
I write this though
I barely know you
To say 'hello' to
though I have sat and listened to your song
great long river tumbling and coursing with language
leaping with huge strange unfamiliar boulders
marram-grass in the sandy wasteland
quartz-pebbles on a sloping beach
grey moustache stained yellow at the edges
laughing, drink in hand, eternal darkred tie
(tractors ploughing white phosphates in the springtime earth through the window)

wanting to plait my song
like you
through the streams and courses of life
to make everyone see
to make everyone know
to change the world

no more poverty
no more dying
no more illness
no more ignorance
'the air curdled with angels'
in the bloodred sunset
over the black islands of your songs.

II

ten child's eyes staring bright at the camera on the Sundaybest settee.

AVRIL   hair in curls from the rags it's rolled up in every night. Me running with her pram up and down the sandhills. thin, shy, loving the cats, frightened of the gascooker. new Civil Service life, flat with Sunday dinner for me and Andy in Nottingham.

TONY   the brother I took for long walks coming back proud bearing tiddlers flashing in the murky jamjar the spring lanes not yet converted to buildersyards. hitchhiking round Europe laying girls in my spare bedroom tired eyes at the dead morning railwaystation.

CHRISTINE   dark beautiful once bitten by the dog now bringing my nephew to see me laughing splashing in the bath. cheeky always in trouble now a nursing-sister in a country hospital.

MICHELLE   brown eyes sunburnt face frilly dress. ponytail teenager dancing at parties kissing on the stairs, married in a little flat high above the busy concrete promenade.

ANDRE   round plump Wimpy face fair hair neatly parted T-shirt patterned with motorcars toy cars and electric roadways patterning the floor now tall buying me pints dancing in discothèques.

me an only lonely child then suddenly a brother. brothers with toy trains bicycles and beer sisters coming to Liverpool for summer dresses or winter popstar concerts. coming home laden with parcels every Christmas. no longer knowing what will surprise them what will please them. Christmas dinner treelights wrappingpaper darkness creeping about with laden stockings making mincepies at 2 a.m. laughing with my mother. long summers of picnics on the beach and home over the humpbacked railwaybridge. new school uniforms we couldn't afford every autumn. spring offensives of whooping cough and measles. always letters from my Mum for money. train tearing me away from my childhood as I write this looking at the full breasts of the girl opposite moving slightly under the pink flowered shirt. September sun on flooded fields. me and André and Tony walking back drunk from the pub after the last funeral weekend. 'Christ, we're orphans' he said, suddenly. we moved on, laughing, empty council-house full of memories waiting for us.

PART TWO 1951–7

1

young
artstudent
under the bridges of Paris
(where else?)
painting badlypainted picturepostcard paintings
Pont des Arts, St-Germain-l'Auxerrois
sketchbook
corduroy elbows on the Pernod table

2

crystalline manna counterpoints the stars
in the deep puddle
frost on gateposts
iridescent
a heavy Williams shadow plunges
blindly between the fuchsias the acacias and the waiting angels
into No. 20, Mon Repos
watched by the lonely poet
midnight dog pissing in the shadows

3

winter evening trickles cold wetness
down black glass between the curtain and the wall

fearing
the stranger's eyes behind your face
when you look too long in the mirror

4

babyfaced   almost thin   N.H.S. glasses
striped college scarf thrown casually over shoulder
various sets of artistic beards and moustaches
learning to drink
Newcastle Brown, Export and Exhibition
Saturdaynight litany of pubs with Alan from the electric train
falling headfirst down a stone colonnade at a Jazz Band Ball
seeing Orphée and Potemkin
waking drunk at 2 a.m. on the roof of someone's house
loving unhappily a greeneyed girl from a mining town
writing adolescent poems of rejection
for something that was never offered
singing on tables and sometimes under them
slipping on a frozen path   the canvas with her portrait
pierced by the stalks of dead chrysanthemums

5

summer loves on the warm concrete promenade
frenzied knickersoff trouserbutton gropings
in the 78 r.p.m. recordplaying frontroom

6

shadowed circle under a summer oaktree at noon
familiar browncheck dress raised high
seeing the strong brown body full for the first time
down the lane past the little yellow house
confident hands guiding me into you

melting elastic beautiful unfamiliar
afterwards sensible scrubbing at dampmarks
hurrying home so your parents won't know

7

O that summer of lightblue eyes and strong brown hands
reflected in black glass café tables
brown El Greco feet running down alleyways of trees
in the Botanical Gardens
home to love summer rain happy down our faces
tasting the rain on your laughing mouth
pink gums above your littlegirl milkteeth
spending our summer wages getting pissed on Fridays
over the iron railway footbridge
kissing goodnight at the end of the semidetached avenue
so your father won't see us
hiding like mice down backstreets when his big black car goes past

8

trying to paint
the Pasmore morning world
of City allotments
striped huts abstract against beanpoles
curling tendrils of branches into mist
patterns of green leaves against conservatory windows
zebrastriped trafficsign city
red triangles
grey distances against the bright trafficlights

9

the library for
Eliot Pound the enchanted islands

Kafka   Auden   MacNeice
Sydney Keyes dead before the foreign gate

and for
the beautiful blonde librarian
round blue eyes   pale face   child's mouth
full fleecy pinksweatered body
round thighs
watched
across afternoon tenniscourts
across morning bookshelves

10

coming back
to our café
black-and-white-tile floor
still the frothiest coffee north of Sorrento
not
the afternoon hangout for the Grammarschool in-crowd
anymore
now
full of babies with red faces
and middleaged mothers
I suddenly realize
were at school with me

11

PRESTON:
rain splattering my glasses
splintering the neonsigns
24   schoolteacher
in a provincial town

12

meeting you
dark noisy club   nomoney dates
home to my flat
remembering
the morning park   the distant railway
the long green caverns in the treefilled square
loving you
in the crowded coffeesmell Kardomah

13

working
as so often
in the noisy blaring fairground
cream-and-red stalls
creampainted rollercoaster against darkblue sky
working
this time with you
brightlycoloured balloons bursting
ROLL 'EM UP   ONE OVER TO WIN   ANY PRIZE YOU LIKE
powderblue nylonfur poodles
against the bright red counter
children crying   runny noses
holidaymakers huddled like sheep under plastic raincoats
from the August rainstorms
coaches revving up in the carpark
ON THE RED THIRTY-THREE   ALL THE THREES THIRTY-THREE
Frankie Laine   Guy Mitchell
loud through the electric nightrides
lights going out running with the heavy shutters
pints with Big Jim and Georgie Lee in the closingtime billiardsroom
fishandchip latenight O'Hara's suppers
concrete promenade still warm under our feet
the long walk home
the Townhall clock and the deserted railwaybridge

14

bright still-lifes
proud yellow lemons red tomatoes
orange-and-white Penguinbooks
blue-and-white mug
painted in the little buildershut I rented
down a lane
furnished with a settee for loving you
an easel for your proud body bright against the yellow walls
down to the Dole on Fridays
fairground closed for the winter
flat red sun   black posts   white seagulls
held whirling
against the darkening sands

15

now
the alleyways and market-gardens
gone
instead huge supermarkets empty as the winter seashore
long shoppers
circling over bargains like seagulls
greeted only by strangers
in the unfamiliar streets

III

saturday morning, reading the lifestory of Dylan Thomas aged 19, coffee in a greenflowered mug, smell of red beans boiling downstairs for Arthur and Carol coming to dinner. my brother and a new girlfriend coming to share the spare bedroom. Sue asleep as always in the big brass bed upstairs. me at the morning desk as always, trying to write something I've been trying to write since June 3rd, 1970, the day my mother died. Tony ringing at 7.45 a.m. me rushing out having to see the bankmanager before getting the train but almost unthinkingly stopping to look for a black tie putting it in my briefcase. he met me at the station and told me the news I'd already guessed dark circles round tired eyes. the last time I saw her in hospital two weeks before, I thought what a beautiful woman she'd been. looking old, thin, wrinkled with illness but the fine cheekbones and forehead there as always. hair bobbed dark against the out-of-focus Florida background of 1930 photos. a blue crêpe dress with a matching summercoat. a darkblue dress with coloured circles like Rowntree's pastilles falling into the distance. not for years the fur coat she always wanted. winesilk danceshoes with diamanté heels. all squashed at the back of the fading wardrobe, in a cardboard box a crushed orangeblossom veil. pushed at the back behind the cheap dresses for the Football Club or the Saturdaynight pub. beautiful young mother holding my hand going for a picnic on the sandhills mysterious to jump off like Sahara now bulldozed into concrete carparks. quick laughing crying emotional quick to read telling me proudly she'd read *Ulysses* in three days. once-a-year concerts of Beethoven. Blake's Grand March or selections from Gounod she'd play on the piano for me. Later there was only the drinking club, dirty joke comedians, the hideous songs from musicals. her bending over beautiful in the darkness to kiss me coming in from a dance smelling of perfume and gin-and-lime. alone, sad, watching the shadows on the ceiling, then loving her watching the rainbows in her necklace as she leaned over me. middleaged, shortsighted, too much effort to read anymore, loving the children's pop songs but still sometimes listening to Caruso and John McCormack. as the children grew older she surrounded herself by cats ramifying family black grey tabby constantly inbreeding. once I used to write home describing every painting I did, everything I wrote. when did I stop? why? suddenly she no longer knew the reason why I did them, only proud of me for the newspaper articles, the television interviews. her ambition, more than perhaps anything else, made me what I am. by the time my first books were published her sight was too bad for her to read them.

Poem for Liverpool 8

LIVERPOOL 8:
blaze of trumpets from basement recordplayers
loud guitars in the afternoon

knowing every inch of little St Bride St
brightgreen patches of mildew redpurple bricks stained ochre plaster
huge hearts names initials kisses painted on backdoors
tiny shop with a lightbulb in the window
Rodney St pavement stretching to infinity
Italian garden by the priest's house
seen through the barred doorway on Catharine St
pavingstones worn smooth for summer feet
St James Rd my first home in Alan's flat
shaken intolerable by Cathedral bells on Sundays
Falkner Sq. Gardens heaped with red leaves to kick in autumn
shuttered yellowgreen with sunlight
noisy with children's laughter in summer
black willows into cold mist
bushes railings pillowed with snow in winter
Gambier Terrace loud Beatle guitars from the first floor
Sam painting beckoning phantoms hiding behind painted words bright colours
in the flooded catfilled basement
pigeons disappearing at eyelevel into the mist
hopscotch-figures vomitstains under my morning feet
Granby St bright bazaars for aubergines and coriander
Blackburne House girls laughing at bus-stops in the afternoon
Blackburne Place redbrick Chirico tower rushing back after love at dinnertime
drunk jammed in the tiny bar in The Cracke
drunk in the crowded cutglass Philharmonic
drunk in noisy Jukebox O'Connor's
smiling landlord on the doorstep huge in shirtsleeves and braces

LIVERPOOL 8:
now a wasteland
murdered by planners not German bombers
crossed by empty roads
drunken lintels falling architraves
Georgian pediments peeling above toothless windows
no Mrs Boyne laughing in the Saturdaynight Greek chipshop
the tumbledown graveyard under the Cathedral

where we kissed behind willowtrees
bulldozed into tidy gardens
huge tornup roots of trees
pink sandstone from uprooted walls glittering in pale sunlight
no happy dirtyfaced children
littering the sidestreets
only a distant echo of their laughter
across the bonfire fireengine debris.

PART THREE 1957–64

1

warm diagonal red-and-black tiles
fire burning in the deep chimneyplace
whitepainted wooden rockingchair   white walls
big regency-striped settee
winter in the little basement yard outside
her voice singing high piping in the kitchen
Saturdaymorning nowork breakfast
reading the *New Statesman*
flames echoing on the low white ceiling

2

blue-and-white-striped mugs
a small stone with holes in smelling of sulphur
we brought home from a beach one day
pueblo-type ashtray from Woolworth's
the sudden apparition, in red,
of the wife of Pierre Bonnard
on the print framed in the alcove
singlebed mattress waiting upright in the tiny wallcupboard
for my hitchhiking friends

3

sharing with you
Bird, Monk or Mingus
Mathis der Maler, Das Lied von der Erde
Little Richard or Muddy Waters for parties
same violin concerto always to go home with
rising upwards beautiful
into the proud cadenza

4

Henry laughing red bearded punning face at parties
climbing the scaffolding on the midnight Cathedral
Don studio floor piled with paint plaster wood
moon landscapes even higher than his paintings
John from America a battered Volkswagen laden with pictures
I met eight years later in a New York bar
Ben from Mayfair exiled to grotty Liverpool
keeping a club for our latenight drunken fantasies

5

Brown   knocking on the 4 a.m. bedroom window
'Psst. It's me,
Brown',
laughing   plaid hitchhiking jacket   full of news
frantic letters for leftbehind poems
or soiled pyjamas

6

Hawkins
ironing his still-drunk trousers to go home to wife and motherinlaw
finding an old clown outfit in the wardrobe

enormous   black   red frills and bobbles
bent over the ironingboard
in the hangover morning

7

on a bus
reading Leopardi, the twisted crookback with the winter's smile
patient broomflower 'upon the shoulder of the arid mountain'
seeing
children filing into school
a young man tweedcoated sadly in the yard, On Duty
wondering
how many exiles to the land of concrete lampposts
the drums and trumpets of success
fading in their ears?

8

still
seeing you on a winter beach
bent forward double from the waist
red jacket black trousers like a wooden soldier
nose tip-tilted
inspecting the sound of barnacles on a lonely post

9

Aldermaston dogs scowling through wire at happy marchers
banners black-and-white against Falcon Field
proud trumpet breaking out over the marching drums
the uphill road   tired legs   feet sore
Joyce and I with the huge wurst sausage
we took every year to eat at roadsides
thrown into horseboxes by grinning policemen on demos

10

now
beginning the time of the infidelities
Carol proud breasts warm everopen mouth
Gail who seduced me in the afternoon newstheatre
Pat
my first schoolgirl love
eating buns on the afternoon ferryboat
carving our names in soft red sandstone
one time encased in plaster
from neck to middle   still feeling your warm body through it
clear blue eyes   darkbrown hair
loving you
even when finding your phonenumber
in someone else's poem

11

seeing
my first Yves Klein
blue universes in a tiny artgallery
lumpen Paolozzi monsters
Newman horizonlight
serene dark Rothko
Robbie the Robot
making 'today's homes
so different, so appealing'

12

DEATH OF A BIRD IN THE CITY
screaming white splattered against windscreen
crucified on a nightdoor
black words running
lost girl giving you dead flowers

last night's blood on tomorrow's pavement
smells of icecream and antiseptic hospitals
poems sweets comics foodpackets
sweet little Chuck Berry schoolgirls
goalposts chalked on greybrick walls
'The Night, Beware of that dark door'
dying among bunches of nightblack flowers
painted screaming unheard in the tarmac city

13

in Philip's photograph
your hair
grown from the littleboy cut now
backcombed round
on a tube train

face and body brown
from the everyday sunbathing whitewashed backyard
dark hair longer still
in another photograph

at the bar
in our favourite club
loving
but not making love

14

painting huge canvases of Piccadilly
Guinness Clock MOTHER'S PRIDE
bright garden   yellow flowers   grey buildings
huge hoardings for eggs or cornflakes
DAFFODILS ARE NOT REAL
scrawled defiantly across the middle
or

at jinglebells Bing Crosby brass band Christmas
Dreaming Of
her pale secret face
behind the cardboard Santaclaus and cutout reindeer

15

moving from Falkner Sq.
thrown out finally after so many times
after the first party
back from our last fairground summer
laughing friends pushing the settee on its castors
round the Square
brave new home
in a Canning St attic

IV

I suppose he was a bit of a failure, really. at least in most people's eyes. he ended
his working life earning a week what I can earn in a night. my mother was always
on at him about money. he'd been a bandleader, a social worker, a jolly uncle in a
holiday camp, a dancing instructor. yet he ended his life as a miserably underpaid
Civil Service clerk in an Army camp near a small seaside town. he'd written a
play, he'd produced plays, he'd run a magazine written by unemployed workers
during the Depression, he'd worked tirelessly to help other people. yet because
he couldn't really help himself we none of us ever really admitted what we felt
about him. it's hard to believe dead people are really dead. the waxwork-yellow
face, the purple-tinged ears in the Chapel of Rest wasn't him. the black hair just
tinged with grey was a cleverly fitted wig. there were Alexandra roses growing
up the redbrick hospital wall outside. my childhood was a border zone where
skirmishes, rocket-attacks, dogfights took place daily. no prisoners taken. 'look
what your mother's done' 'did you hear what your father said'. a lonely observer,
fired on by both sides at once. when the children grew up and they withdrew
behind their own lives it was too late for him to stop. he used to complain inces-
santly, often to himself, shuffling about in the kitchen or the garden, a Cassandra

in a shabby blue suit, a Jeremiah with no tribe to listen, a shepherd-boy constantly muttering 'wolf', a forgotten Coriolanus in voluntary exile. still a handsome man even into his sixties, black sleekback 1930s hair always chatting up the prettiest girl at the party. after he died we found a Last Will and Testament amongst his things. the name and address and date were filled in. the rest was left blank.

Poem for Summer 1967

I think perhaps the thing I've envied most
is my aunts' easy tears at funerals
crying for someone they hardly knew and hadn't seen for years
I can't cry for anyone
not really
tears come readily
at the thought of justice or injustice
when they came and put out our bonfire when I was a child
reading Nicola Sacco's last letter
seeing the triumphant crowd bearing banners into the distance
invading tanks and flowers on bloodstained pavements
heard on the noisy foreign radio
not you dying
but the stupid cheap chords of hymns at funerals
brought the tears to my eyes

Scott McKenzie singing 'San Francisco'
nostalgic now further away than The White Cliffs of Dover
long soft body in her husband's bed
walking to the bank in the nextday hangover rain
crowded noisy party
Tony and I picking nasturtiums for our hair
in the darksmelling summer garden
faraway summer gone for ever
thunderclouds massing   mist on trees   flooded fields through hedges
Canning Street polished flooboards home
sideboard elaborate   brickwashed wall above brass fireplace

bedroom collaged with posters to hide where the rain came in
black cat jumping through skylight on to the bed
polish worn away by so many footsteps
so many different faces on the pillow
painting bright salads
meat oozing red electric in the neonlight
tiny universes of cream cakes
clean white canvas waiting ambiguous
Allen singing washing the morning dishes
Bob Creeley laughing at the cardboard I put in my shoes to keep the rain out
Sunday morning sunfilled Albert Dock with Jonathan

Kissing warm snuggled like childbed
Kissing autumn eyes welling up in the darkened hallway
Kissing away from your best friend under every secret streetlamp

flat now empty
Joyce two streets away room with dried rushes and butterflies

laths fractured sticking through falling plaster
wet paper flapping
rain dripping monotonous
broken-tiled steps to the peeling doorway.

PART FOUR SUMMER 1970

1

moving
once again
strange new worlds of limegreen carpet
cat not knowing where to sleep unfamiliar
doors banging at night apprehensive
downstairs every morning to the windowdesk

schoolgirls laughing beautiful past at 3.45 p.m. daily
blue-and-white dishes
in the evening kitchen

2

Rites of Spring
celebrated in a bluecarpeted room
looking on to the treefilled square
grey spring sky tangled in my fingers with your blonde hair
running my mouth down your warm wet body
the night we had to climb a ladder to your bedroom

3

wind moving high in the summer trees
blowing away the wasp that's near my hand
a tiny yellowgreen insect walking across the blue lines of this paper
poppies in the tall grass
camomile and dead nettles swaying
farmgate open
fields of rye rippling in waves
smell of tar from the newlaid road
bright yellow light behind my closed eyes
last year's leaves blowing in the sunlight

4

you
the Yorkshire Poacher
singing over metal nests
two buttering happy
for breakfast
smelling the toasthaze drifting
between the cooker and the door

5

purple loosestrife at the edge of the bay
sea flat grey into the distance
early blackberry flowering along the marshes
tiny troutbeck streams struggling through boulders
soft green hills divided by blackstone walls

warm young body under crimson sweater
patched blue jeans you washed specially for today
wind blowing towards us from the dark mills at the end of streets
warm mouth warm kisses cold hands cold wind
on the station platform

eating Chinese food afterwards waterchestnut crunching in my mouth
remembering crisp white teeth
still feeling your soft body against my chest under my arm
eyes wide amazed at the newness of things
alone on your bike in the 3 a.m. newspaper streets
holding my hand on a summer afternoon
writing poems on your examination papers

flocks of wild geese moving across the lake
loving you in frozen silences of fern and rhododendron
the pathway by the water alive with baby frogs
sharing your wonder at the tiny life jumping to escape
from your cupped hands

6

NORWAY:
parked in the middle of the most beautiful landscape in the world
a green-and-red van with SPORTY FORD painted on it
clear viridian depths of cold rivers
waterfalls veiling the sides of granite mountains
last year's snow unmelted   their sides blotting into the mist

laughing blonde girls picking brightpink flowers
old man waiting between the clock and the bed
white birdwings against green fields
small boats lapping at the fiord's edge
unwanted painting
left in the snow outside the painter's cottage

7

you
dreaming of being a salmon
in a lake of crystal water
the scales and dripping waterbeads
changing into a princess's garments
tightfitting hat crusted with rubies and diamonds
trapped by wicked gnomes
in the long grass
across the field
on the way to find the treasure
in the secret garden

8

your familiar voice
on the telephone
happy to type the poems I write for other people
happy to hold the body I give to other people
welcoming me warm into you
happy to make our onenight home in other people's bedrooms

9

rust-red rowanberries
against the rustred roof
of an old barn

inside the warmsmelling hay stacked into darkness
scrambling through tiny streams
clear to the marble fragments on the bottom
ferns higher than your head
dead goose crucified on a bright green cowfield
sudden blood   ribcage   white feathers scattered
small dog jumping for the wildflowers in my hand
a cowman shouting and whistling
across the valley
evening falling
only a trout jumping to break the yellowgreen silence

10

you
in the foreground
farmyard
feeding the ducks
and ducklings
hens and chickens
3 white geese
about your feet

11

living in all my London homes
from home
brokenbacked bedsettee   tiny bed in Ted's spare room
big basement bed in Windmill Hill
arguing with Christopher in a pub
trying to purify the dialectician of the tribe
afternoon wine in Bernard's shop
summer haunted by breasts and minithighs
remembered eyes among rush-hour faces

12

Hampstead   aeroplane garden morning
6 a.m. pale gold bedroom daylight
curtains of honeysuckle and wistaria
darkgreen figleaves
modestly concealing the sky
delicate pink light through climbing roses
morning birdsong   the noise of beginning traffic
pears falling soundlessly from heavy branches
Sunday kites high in the clear air
trees   grass   lakes laid out neatly for inspection

13

you
as Little Nemo
across the magic bridge to Slumberland
curled up sleeping on a bedsettee
in the Palace of King Morpheus

the Girl from Porlock
calling me downstairs from writing this poem
to watch you laughing lying back
in our new bathroom
house full of treasures
you display proudly from the market every Saturday

14

along the churchyard
rhododendron   magnolia
distant bell
path I walked with her as a child
to her mother's grave
dead redandwhite flowers
lashed by the rain as I write

15

after the empty years between
suddenly given
the literary
lion's share
but who
to share it with?
the lion sleeps
confused, exhausted.
the dark outside echoes to his cries.

Tea with the Poet

We are going to tea with a poet.
Confidences poured out –
'One lump or two? Milk?'
– and passed round the table.
Hot toasted paragraphs
dripping with melted adjectives,
sentences with the crusts neatly cut off,
a tempting selection of metaphors –
'Must watch the figure'
– laid out on a plate for us to choose from.

It is teatime with the poet.
'A second cup? Certainly.
Pass the haiku. A villanelle?
Go on, spoil yourself.
Sure you haven't got room for a sonnet?
Oh, very well.'

Time to go.
He brushes up a few commas from the tablecloth
and, with a polite semi-colon;
shows us to the door.

Poet in School

'Write about
something that's happened to you
or someone you know.' Half an hour
to go, and still nothing written.
Just sitting, face blank as the empty sheet,
shuffling his feet. 'Come on, son,
you must know something that's happened
to someone.' 'No, Sir.'
'Your family, your friends?'
'Sir, my brother's best mate died.'
'How?' 'Sir, electrocuted. A train…'
'Was he on the track?' 'Sir…'
The empty eyes fill with tears.
Somehow the years between us
aren't enough to take the words back.

Back Gardens

That morning regret
yet again;
seeing from a train
patios and greenhouses,
bright plastic toys,
carousels of washing,
satellite-discs and rockeries,
louvred garage doors:
nostalgia for a vanished world
I never knew.

The Image

It is the dark tunnel
with nightmare orange lights
It is the voice on the radio
saying there is a change to the advertised programme
It is the taste of a tear
in front of the lunchtime T.V. news
It is the sound of rain on cellophane
round pink and white carnations
It is the patient shuffling of lines of umbrellas
It is a child's praying hands
against a blue school sweatshirt
It is a wreath of white plastic chrysanthemums
in a Liverpool shop window
In the endless clicking of shutters
it is the final image
That you will not see
That no one can take away from you
It is the minute's silence
at the end of the poem.

Aubade, Ward E

1

Striped nurses
slip silent into lighted tents
whisper words within
like clandestine lovers

2

A Saxon burial-figure
I lie in bed, knees to chest,
but apart. Hands across heart
Poulenc's Piano Concerto l
looping through my head.

3

Where do they go to?
Where not go gentle?
Coughing, farting, retching,
shuffling, into below-flight-deck
neon light, airport air
tinged with the smell of the mahonia
from Christine's garden.

4

I want to be
in a dark warm place with you,
where no-one can hear me say
'I love you'. Where I would slip between
your breath, where we would float,
between the notes, beyond the Isle of Capri,
where pain melts away
into gentle day.

The Hours of the Insomniac

How terrifying it is in the night,
the convex face of the black land
Bertolt Brecht, 'The First Psalm'

um Mitternacht
after the T.V. is turned off
before the whistling hour begins
afraid of the dark forest
huddled in the bedtime dark for comfort
switch on the light
on the unnecessary landing
even before the tiny bright dot fades

picking at the scar-tissue of memory
shades of abandoned projects
things put off till tomorrow
phonecalls not made
poems unwritten
rise like Bosworth at the bedside
'Despair and die…'
dusty folders exhumed
then reinterred mingle
with cries of night club goers
howl of car alarms
crunch of past daydreams
the sound of smashed windscreens

ice-floes piled horizontal
have pushed through the bedroom window
snowflakes drift into the room
settle on the dark green sheets
melt on your warm body
a polar bear pokes its snout
through the yellow curtains
decides to ignore us.

It is the wreck of hope.
Beneath the glaucous sky
a muffled sentry plods tireless
through the snow
along the lamplit street.

Standing on the edge
of the Great Grimpen Mire
one incautious word
to betray the innocent clumps of green
lost behind The Wall
one casual gesture enough
to call down the waiting Stasi, VoPo,
grey-clad GrePo.

Three o'clock:
the plump, manicured hand
that tears my shadow from the wall
crumples it into a ball
discarded
on the green-carpeted floor

garden-gnomes roam
sinister in the gloaming

in the dark night of the soul
it is always 4 a.m.
hobbling at dawn
along the verge of a foreign motorway
wandering weeping down Devon lanes

you wake
a stranger
turn away from me
a stranger
warm back an ocean away

5.00
familiar red bedside glow

the wrong footpath
ending high on the castle walls
lost turnings, the wrong staircase
wrong words, lost clothes
interminable detours to the wrong station
helpless at night at the end of the line
futile panic, the desperate lunge
for forgotten poems, locked corridors,
inaccessible stage
blind in the spotlights
sickening lurch at the edge of the abyss
where the yellow lines and tarmac end

5.05: criminal shadows. Slow march of red digits

and sometimes the balm
calm as distant nocturnes
the amen of sunlight
catching gold motes
on cold river water
breath grasping the body
the roundness of pebbles
loving clench of red mud
between the toes

as the moon sets
over the temple of the past
images squeak and gibber
in the sheeted dark
flicker, circle endlessly,
like goldfish

your phantom smell beneath the bedclothes

real as the half-dreamt knocking
on the 6 a.m. door

tender keloid of memory
preserved in black amber
dawn chorus of police sirens
keyboard-chatter of rain
tired brain disputes the claim
of morning

Eight o'clock.

the light
is the colour of the tears
that squeeze from beneath
your closed eyelids.

Je Suis un Autre

> *Je est un autre.*
> Arthur Rimbaud

This is not my face
this owlish staring
pair of eyes
this is not my face
not my body
the gnarled hands
the hands of a stranger
the shard of flesh
hanging beneath my belly
the useless rage

This is not my mind
someone else's mind

someone who knows
the same things I know
but knows them differently
this constant useless
barrage of information
songs that only I could know
songs from my childhood
things we did at school
forties pop songs
rise unbidden from my head
erasing all other thoughts
Is it always like this?

Inside that total stranger
I am the withered stranger
they have taken away
They left this poor pathetic fragment
in disguise, in replacement
Who are you?
Why are you watching?
What are you thinking?
I only know that I am
becoming you, that your body
is slowly taking over my mind
my body taking over your body

I am not you
I am me somewhere
somewhere in the darkness
lying, abandoned
until then, it is just you
Je est un autre
Je suis un autre

Durham Poem

Je me souviens.
Georges Pérec

Walking up the path
of your mother's garden
I slipped, and the portrait
I was doing of you
under the depth
of the lilac bushes
was pierced.
I remember you
were wearing a turquoise circular skirt
other than that
I remember your face
smiling miraculously out
of the ruin of the picture.
I remember the night train
the electric train
on Saturdays
the old guard train.
Central Station to King's College
always by a different route.
Most of the pubs now gone. Will Curley,
run by the Bare Fist Champion of Europe,
his pub alongside the market.
In the dim light
pictures of boxers on the wall.
You only drank halves and
they came from the cellar.
They all seemed so big.
Mercer, majestically drunk, waving across
the crowded bun room
two quarts of Newcastle Light Ale
in either pocket
always, I notice,

symmetrical.
Saturday afternoon in St James's Park
Haway the lads, 'wor Jackie'.
Once, sitting on a train
and a little boy saying to his big sister
'Is Jackie Milburn the Prime Minister?'
Jesmond Dene in the snow,
Euston Road landscapes transported
to the North of England.
Walking to Cullercoats on Sunday morning
to the pub
and coming back in time for lunch.
The little harbour swept clear
and bright by the incoming tide.
Poised on a rock, the cathedral
rising like a reproach,
gothic, beautiful, rising
above the waters
gothic, wonderful,
that I could never surmount.
How I envied the rowing boats
and the rowers,
so effortless
beneath the ground.
Finally to come back to the place
where the painting was ruined
in the garden. And, and somehow we both,
and somehow to evoke that time, that place,
that mystery.

Buckinghamshire
ARTS
SSOCIATION

55 High Street, Aylesbury, Bucks HP20 1SA
Aylesbury (0296) 434704

BOOK.THE WRITER

CLAIM FOR REIMBURSEMENT

REPORT BY ORGANISER (which must be completed before subsidy is released)

Please comment on the visit made by the writer named overleaf, with reference
to the format of the visit, audience response, arrangements, and whether you
would wish to invite this writer again. Details of any variation which had to
be made to the visit should also be noted.

```
Name of Writer:   Adrian Henri

Date of Visit:

Establishment: Little Kingshill Co. Co.
                                  School
Age-Range of Audience:
                       11+ & 12+
Number Attending:
                  60
Signed: France, Eliasly  Date: 8/5/87
```

Mr. Adrian Henri was punctual.

His talk was lively, imaginative and informative - enjoyed by

both adults and children.

Unfortunately his personal appearance left much to be desired and

did nothing to reinforce the standards of dress and hygiene held within

the school.

It also did nothing to improve the image of Liverpool, a city in

need of ambassadors.

Index of First Lines